VOGUEPRENEURS

VOGUEPRENEURS

WOMEN ENTREPRENEURS WHO HAVE BUILT MILLION-DOLLAR BRANDS THROUGH DIGITAL PLATFORMS

ANDREA SIRACUSE

NEW DEGREE PRESS

VOGUEPRENEURS

Women entrepreneurs who have built million-dollar brands through digital platforms

ISBN   978-1-63676-505-1   *Paperback*

        978-1-63676-023-0   *Kindle Ebook*

        978-1-63676-024-7   *Ebook*

For my husband, Stu. Thank you for always believing in me.

CONTENTS

———

You will fail.

It's inevitable.

It's what you do with it.

-J.K. ROWLING

A NEW WAVE OF DIGITAL WOMEN ENTREPRENEURS

———

It's the year 2015. I'm in my 600 sq ft apartment in the nation's capital, getting ready for a night out with my girls. As I'm putting the final touches on my face, I'm having the hardest time covering my pimples. Everything I currently have is either too cakey, or I need to use half the bottle to have a face worthy of a night out. Frustrated by my options, I start researching a foundation that is lightweight; something you can barely feel with enough coverage for a natural looking finish. After about 5 minutes of searching the interweb, I stumble upon Glossier's Perfecting Skin Tint. I'd heard of Glossier, but I'd never tried any of its products. That would soon change.

With over a dozen blog posts on why this skin-tinter foundation is a must-have for your daily beauty lineup, I had to order it. When it arrived, I was shocked at how little

I needed to use to achieve an all-natural look while still covering up my blemishes. From that point on, I was forever grateful to Emily Weiss, the founder of Glossier, for creating a product like this. Eternal brand loyalty: locked. I will forever stand with Emily Weiss. May the beauty gods forever bless her soul.

This wasn't the first time anyone had whipped out an iPhone to find a beauty product. The truth is, we turn to our digital devices, whether to look at reviews before we purchase something or to text friends and family, asking what they use.

We've transitioned from a culture of bloggers, "It" girls, and celebrities into powerful, lucrative "influencers" within a decade. Many think of influencers as valley girls with lots of money who post their pretty pictures on Instagram, but truthfully, that's selling them short.

I define influencers as a new wave of entrepreneurs for our time.

These are people with the ability to build a community of followers and influence the purchasing decisions of millions.

Brands partner with influencers—who can make upwards of five thousand dollars per photo or review—to post on their social channels. Thanks to the platform, (they gain from brand partnerships on their channels) influencers are now building their own brands and creating their own products. They know what types of products their audience loves, and they're able to profit off of it.

As a consumer, I've become a sucker for purchasing new products I find on Instagram; anyone close to me will tell you it's true. I love discovering new influencers on social media. As I enter my thirties, the things I care most about and my lifestyle are changing, and so are the people I follow on my social media accounts. My feed is no longer general ads for clothing and beauty products; it's more personal. Influencers create a deep, trusting connection with their followers, so influencers who go on create their own brand already have a loyal following, releasing products that their followers believe they absolutely cannot live without (looking at you, Emily Weiss).

I've become attached—not stage-five clinger attached—but obsessed enough to drive to Macy's (a store I've never shopped at) to purchase a product from an influencer that just launched her first collection (more on this later). You get the point. People who we've never met and who we wake up with every day have become our friends (literally, I sleep next to my phone at night so it's the same thing, right? I'm such a millennial).

Think of an influencer you love. This is someone you relate to; the content they post is funny, they're authentic, you love their style, and the list goes on. You're now in their corner, rooting for their success. When they drop an announcement about a new partnership or collection, you're the first one in line with your credit card. That's how I feel about the women in this book.

Having grown up in this digital world (well, since I owned my first Motorola Razr flip phone back in 2006), I've followed these women's careers since their starts. When they got their first big deal or collaboration, I eagerly waited for their product(s) to come out and wanted to contribute to the success of these self-starters. These women created their own path, breaking the traditional ways marketing has been done in the past, all while setting new exceptions on how we create, promote, and market products.

From the outside looking in, it appears that anyone can become an influencer and create a brand online. It must be easy: free vacations, free meals, free outfits, and upwards up five thousand dollars per post, amiright?

Trust me, it's not easy. I am a social media manager, so I know what I'm talking about. I've learned how brands undervalue influencer partnerships and don't fully understand how influencers can help them grow.

As influencers become more plentiful and proven, brand dollars have flooded into the new industry. Brands are set to spend up to fifteen billion dollars on influencer marketing by 2022, per *Business Insider* Intelligence estimates and based on Mediakix data.[1] Brands not taking part are losing out. Businesses are making $5.20 for every $1 spent on influencer marketing.[2] That stat alone should encourage you to look into how you could leverage your own digital presence as a side hustle to make extra cash. A 2019 survey by The Influencer Marketing Hub (partnering with Viral Nation

---

1   "The Influencer Marketing Report," Business Insider, accessed March 28, 2020.

2   "Influencer Marketing Stats | 80 Influencer Marketing Statistics For 2020," Influencer Marketing Hub, accessed March 28, 2020.

and NeoReach) emphasizes how influencer marketing can be highly lucrative. Eighty-four percent of companies plan on working with a social media star in the next year. Collaborating with a digital influencer is now one of the most trusted and effective ways for brands to reach consumers.[3]

During my nearly seven years working in social media, I've helped dozens of brands, such as Visit the Outer Banks, MyEyeDr., Amazon, and Marriott International. I now work as a social media manager at a tech company focused in healthcare, based out of North Carolina. I've helped brands from all sizes (from Fortune 500 to small and medium-sized companies) shape their social strategy and grow their community base. I've seen influencer partnerships go right, and I've seen many go wrong. However, companies utilizing influencer marketing often get positive results.

But, what about when partnerships go wrong? The bottom twenty-five fail to generate any revenue.[4]

THOSE ARE THE FIRMS THAT:
- Don't fully understand the mechanics of influencer marketing and
- Didn't do their research.

Businesses not benefiting from influencer marketing are selecting the wrong influencers for their brand.

---

3   Ibid.
4   Ibid.

Typically, they fail to choose influencers who have a follower demographic similar to their own target market for the brand's product. Influencers can become super successful on their social media platforms using a common formula to grow and influence a community.

This book tells the story of my favorite businesswomen and influencers, how they grew their brands, and how they made a living doing it. The women in this book are badass. I love them, not just for the products they created or their partnerships, but because I've grown up with them. These women have been telling their story in their own ways by giving their audience relatable and aspirational content that people want to follow. Without the rise of digital, we wouldn't have that quick of access into their lives.

I want to share these women's stories, including my own, because although I haven't met them in real life, they have made me and so many others feel connected to them by listening to us and creating products for us.

We'll take a deep dive into why these influencers have been so successful in building a personal brand and turning that brand into a company. We'll take a look at the history of how we got here: how "blogger" became "influencer" and how the "It" girls of Hollywood turned their socialite status into a way to express global, influential power over a digital community. And, we'll look at stories from when I was living in Washington, D.C., trying to make it as an influencer and why it didn't work.

This isn't a book about how to be an influencer. Rather, it's a book about women entrepreneurs, influencers, and the intersection of the two.

There are great lessons and takeaways to learn from each profile, which can be summarized by the Four S Process:

- **SPARK**: How each influencer sparked an idea,
- **SOCIAL MEDIA**: How she used digital to extend her reach and grow her community of followers,
- **SECRET SAUCE**: How she blazed a trail for herself in an industry that wasn't accepting applications, and
- **SUCCESS**: How she turned it all into a successful business.

If you love reading about women's success stories in the beauty and fashion industries and how they used digital to build a name for themselves and make millions using platforms like Instagram, find a cozy spot on the couch (in your comfiest sweatpants) and let me take you on a journey with some of **the biggest bosses throughout the beauty and fashion industry.**

PART 1

THE BEGINNING

CHAPTER 1

HISTORY OF DIGITAL

———

It is the early 2000s and my teenage self is dancing and twirling to whatever music is playing on MTV.

I was fourteen years old and without a license, so in my free time I turned to music and, of course, Total Request Live (TRL). If you don't know what TRL is, I'm sorry. It was seriously the best show on MTV, and I'm devastated it doesn't exist anymore. Carson Daly, the host of TRL, was my dream man: tall, dark and handsome. TRL was a place to learn new music, listen, and watch music videos. I was obsessed with it.

I could be caught any time of day with my Walkman (for my gen-z readers, this is how we listened to music) on my hip, singing in the mirror while watching TRL. I would put on my sassiest outfit (think feathers, lots of pink, and sequins on every seam in every outfit) and makeup covering every inch of my face, including hot pink glitter eyeshadow that made me look like a backup dancer for Christina Aguilera. It was a look.

I loved dancing and dressing the part back then. My parents even have home videos of me with dance routines to various music with friends. It was a normal Saturday afternoon activity for me.

Whenever new releases came out, I would beg my mom to take me to RadioShack as soon as it opened. I would wait in line (no matter how long it took) to get whatever new album was the hottest hit at the time. After all, I could only get updates about an album release via the radio or television (mainly TRL). My mom said I was too young to watch TRL, but I sneak-watched MTV whenever I could. There was no "network" of people to connect with that had the same interests as me. All I knew is whatever the television or radio host wanted me to know. That's all the information I had.

It's hard to imagine a time before social media. Back in the nineties, we would get information through televisions, magazines, radio stations, billboards, friends, and family. We now simply pick up our phone and can Google anything we want. The evolution of digital content has skyrocketed over the years, especially in the last thirty years. If someone were to land on earth today and ask me to help them get acquainted to this world, I would literally hand them an iPhone and say, "Here you go! This is where you should start."

For the 4.57 billion internet users worldwide consuming digital content, we all know and use it as part of our everyday routine.[5] Through our phones and computers, we're able to get news, purchase goods, listen to music, and connect with friends and family living across the world. We're able to learn

---

5   "Digital Users Worldwide 2020 | Statista," Statista, accessed March 28, 2020.

and do things that we've never been able to do before. It's crazy to think smartphones have only been around for a little over a decade now. No more waiting in long lines to purchase that new lipstick you heard about from a friend or waiting by the TV to see your favorite brand release a new product you can't wait to try. Our world has been completely transformed by our new ability to market, sell, and purchase online—a transformation propelled by social media.

Before we really get into how digital has played such an important role through the stories of women in this book, let's take a look at some of the major digital milestones that have completely transformed our world into a digital one.

We'll focus on the main digital channels that have helped the women we are spotlighting become influencers and successful businesswomen.

1997

SIXDEGREES.COM LAUNCHED

I honestly completely forgot about Six Degrees. This platform was known (probably to very few of you) as the first social media platform. In reality, it was basically a glorified address book. Think of it as a webpage of contacts for your family and friends. It was named after the six degrees of separation concept and allowed users to list friends, family members, and acquaintances both on the site and externally; external contacts were invited to join the site.[6] People who confirmed a relationship with an existing user, but did not go on to

---

6   Ibid.

register with the site, continued to receive occasional email updates and solicitations. Users could send messages and post bulletin board items to people in their first, second, and third degrees, and see their connection to any other user on the site.

Six Degrees, at one point, had around one hundred employees and around three-and-a-half million fully registered members. The site was purchased by YouthStream Media Networks in December 1999 for one-hundred-and-twenty-five million dollars.[7] 🙈

AOL INSTANT MESSENGER

I didn't have a Six Degrees account, but I spent most of my teenage years chatting with friends and boyfriends on AIM. For all my eighties and nineties babies, do you remember changing your away status to something like "maybe...ur gonna b the 1 that saves me...brb shower" when you broke up with your boyfriend? Or changing your profile to music lyrics depending on your current mood? I think my screen name was something to do with princess and glitter?

AIM was popular from the late 1990s to the late 2000s in North America and was the leading instant messaging application in that region. AIM's popularity declined steeply in the early 2010s as internet social networks like Twitter gained

---

7 "COMPANY NEWS; YOUTHSTREAM TO ACQUIRE SIXDEGREES FOR $125 MILLION," Nytimes.com, accessed March 28, 2020.

popularity, and its fall has often been compared with the once-popular internet service Myspace. [8]

2000

SIXDEGREES.COM SHUT DOWN

Google.com launched in 1998, four years after Yahoo.com. Could you imagine being a student at Stanford University and announcing you wanted to build a website where you could literally search ANYTHING in the whole world? Well, Sergey Brin, an American software engineer, teamed up with Larry Page, another PhD student at Stanford, to start Google in September 1998. [9]

When I think of Google, I think of Google Docs, Google Calendar, Google Slides, Google Home—pretty much anything I need to help me keep everything organized and on track. Google products aren't just designed for personal use but have helped millions of small businesses as well. Google has Google Analytics to see how your website traffic is doing, Google AdWords to reach more people, and even can create personal template invoices (it's so cool if you have a small business, and you should check it out if you don't know what I'm talking about). I guess that's how you become the most visited website in the world.

---

8   "The Rise And Fall Of AIM, The Breakthrough AOL Never Wanted," Mashable, accessed March 28, 2020.

9   "'Google Was Not A Normal Place': Brin, Page, And Mayer On The Accidental Birth Of The Company That Changed Everything," Vanity Fair, accessed March 28, 2020.

2002

LINKEDIN LAUNCHED

This company was founded in December 2002 by Reid Hoffman and former employees of PayPal and Socialnet.com.[10] Initially, LinkedIn was used as a business—an employment-oriented social networking service that operated via websites and mobile apps. It's now mainly used for professional networking, including employers posting jobs and job-seekers posting their CVs. As of 2015, the company's revenue came from selling access to information about its members to recruiters and sales professionals.

LinkedIn currently has 706+ million users in more than two hundred countries around the world since May, 2020.[11] It's definitely not a channel I went to first in the past, but as LinkedIn grows (Microsoft reported that LinkedIn's revenue grew 24 percent in Q2 2020) it's becoming a place to show your thought leadership.[12] This channel is now used by a lot of experts in their field, showcasing their professional beliefs and providing a professional resource on their networks. For example, sponsored InMail (a way to send personalized messages to people who matter most to your business) has a 52 percent open rate, on average.[13] If you're in B2B marketing, there's no doubt your LinkedIn business strategy is already in full swing.

---

10   "About LinkedIn," LinkedIn.com, accessed March 28, 2020.
11   Ibid.
12   "16 LinkedIn Statistics That Matter to Marketers in 2019," Social Media Marketing & Management Dashboard, accessed March 28, 2020.
13   "Sponsored InMail Best Practices & Gallery of Examples," accessed August 30, 2020.

For the first time, if you have a profile on LI, you're able to message and network with people in a professional setting, digitally.

2003

MYSPACE LAUNCHED

I can't believe I'm admitting this, but I was never on Myspace (I know!). I never really had the urge to join, but maybe it was because a lot of my friends at the time weren't on the channel? I'll never know. I was more into AOL online chatting.

This is the year social media takes off.

WORDPRESS GOES LIVE

Now, anyone with a computer can write a blog post. This was a huge moment for a lot of people. You're now able to reach more people with your stories, thoughts, and ideas.

Also, during this time frame, Mark Zuckerburg develops "FaceMash." Before Facebook was Facebook, Zuckerburg set up a "hot or not" online game. Harvard students could compare photographs of other students side-by-side and vote for who they thought was better looking.

2004

"FaceMash" is completely transformed into what we know as Facebook.

To think of some college student in his dorm room collecting data and photos of people to compare who is hotter is disturbing, so we'll just note it here and move on...

FACEBOOK IS BORN

Facebook was quickly on its way to becoming the hub of all social media channels and the mega of mega social media platforms. I remember a time when I was so jealous I couldn't have access to Facebook yet because it was only for college students. Wow, have times changed.

2005

YOUTUBE IS CREATED

This was the first platform to introduce video sharing in a way that made it easy to watch online videos. The first YouTube video, "Me at the Zoo," was uploaded by co-founder Jawed Karim. The video documents his day at the San Diego Zoo and is quite awkward if you Google it.

2006

TWITTER LAUNCHED

When Twitter was founded on July 15, 2006, it was launched as a short messaging service for groups to share with the public. Users could share these short updates with groups of friends by sending one text message to a single number: "40404."[14]

---

14   "The Real History Of Twitter - Business Insider," Business Insider, accessed March 28, 2020.

It reminds me of one big open text message to both your friends and the world. The first tweet was posted by founder Jack Dorsey. It read "just setting up my twttr." Over the next few years, Twittr became Twitter, the simple "microblogging" service that allowed you to share quick, simple thoughts with anyone (that is, thoughts that fit under one-hundred-and-forty characters).

During this year, Facebook also launched its new feed.

2007

IPHONE LAUNCHED

A touchscreen phone with an iPod, camera, web-browsing capabilities—we all know how much this moment changed our digital landscape forever.

TUMBLR LAUNCHED

This American microblogging and social networking website was founded by David Karp in 2007 and is currently owned by Automattic. The service allows users to post multimedia and other content to a short-form blog. Users can follow other users' blogs. Bloggers can also make their blogs private. For bloggers, many of the website's features are accessed from a "dashboard" interface.

2009

Facebook surpassed Myspace as the most-visited social media website. [15]

---

15   "Facebook Overtakes MySpace in U.S.," PCWorld, accessed March 28, 2020.

With the introduction of live feed, the company also took a competitive swing at the growing popularity of Twitter. Similar to Twitter's ongoing stream of user posts, live feed pushed posts from friends automatically to a member's homepage. (Live feed has since been incorporated into news feed.)

2010

INSTAGRAM IS CREATED

Instagram is the home for visual storytelling for everyone from celebrities, newsrooms and brands, to teens, musicians, and anyone with a creative passion.

I still remember my first Instagram post. It was a photo of my English bulldog named Carlton. I loved how I was able to edit my photo within the app and upload it, similarly to Facebook, for my friends to see. I also loved how Instagram's platform was easy to use and had a clean, visual appeal.

PINTEREST LAUNCHED

Pinterest is a platform for a visual bookmarking and a tool that helps you discover and save creative ideas.

2011

DIGITAL BOOM

This was a big year for digital. Web use surpassed television use among younger audiences between the ages of eighteen and twenty-nine, a study from the Pew Research Center reports. 65 percent of people younger than thirty cited the internet as their go-to source for news, nearly doubling from 34 percent in 2007. [16]

SNAPCHAT IS LAUNCHED

This photo and video app was launched in 2011 by Evan Spiegel, Eggiest Brown, and Bobby Murphy, all students at Stanford. The site has three-hundred-and-sixty million active monthly users, as of January 2020, with three billion "snaps" sent every day. [17]

Snapchat started video sharing that other platforms took notice in (hint: Instagram). This social channel allowed users to share video content directly to friends. It was most popular for its quick videos you could send to friends that only latest for ten seconds and instantly disappeared.

2012

FACEBOOK PURCHASED INSTAGRAM.[18]

Say what?! I remember when I first heard this. In Facebook's largest acquisition to date, the social network purchased Instagram, the popular photo-sharing application, for about one billion dollars in cash and stock. This was a HUGE purchase, and I feel like, if Instagram was up for grabs today, it would be worth billions.

---

16   "Internet Surpasses Television as Main News Source for Young Adults [STUDY]," Mashable, accessed March 28, 2020.

17   "A Brief History of Snapchat," Hubspot.Com, accessed March 28, 2020.

18   "Facebook Buys Instagram for $1 Billion," DealBook, accessed March 28, 2020.

TAILORED ADS ON FACEBOOK.
Facebook, within the same year, unveiled new advertising opportunities for brands, allowing ads to mix in with Facebook status updates and photos.[19] This was a huge deal for businesses as well as influencers, who could now use these tools to build their brand.

Think of it as a way to now serve your content to people who are actually interested in your business. If you were to advertise on a billboard, you'd have no idea who is seeing that ad, what age group viewed it the most, and so on. Facebook's targeted ads allow you to customize your ads based on criteria like age, interests, geography, and more.

2013
VINE LAUNCHED
Vine was founded by Dom Hofmann, Rus Yusupov, and Colin Kroll in June, 2012. The company was acquired by Twitter in October, 2012 for a reported thirty million dollars, but was later reformed as Intermedia Labs. Vine launched on January 24, 2013, as a free app for iOS devices. An Android version was released on June 2, 2013.

In 2013, Vine began allowing users to record clips with their phones' front-facing cameras, and usage exploded. An ecosystem of young stars sprung up around the service, which evolved into a kind of live-action CartoonNetwork. There was Zach King, who's eye-popping magic tricks earned him

---

19 "Timeline: Key Dates in Facebook's 10-Year History." Phys.Org, accessed March 28, 2020.

four million followers and more than 1.4 billion views.[20] Or Amanda Cerny, who's physical comedy earned more than 2.2 billion views. Logan Paul, who's Vines looped more than four billion times, parlayed his following into a series of acting roles—while earning as much as two-hundred thousand dollars to create a single Vine for a brand, according to a recent *60 Minutes* report. [21]

Former executives say that a major competitive challenge emerged when Instagram introduced fifteen-second video clips in June, 2013.[22] "Instagram video was the beginning of the end," one former executive told me. "Vine didn't move fast enough to differentiate." Instagram courted celebrities with longer videos, eventually bumping the limit to a more flexible sixty seconds. (Vines didn't break the six-second barrier until earlier that year, and its extended videos never caught on.) Instagram also began promoting celebrity accounts in its popular "explore" tab, bringing them attention that Vine found difficult to match. Marketers began shifting their money away from Vine, and stars followed.[23]

On December 16, 2016, it was announced that the Vine mobile app would remain operational as a standalone service, allowing users to publish their videos directly to Twitter

---

20 "Why Vine Died," The Verge, accessed March 28, 2020.

21 Ibid.

22 "Facebook Announces Video for Instagram," The Verge, accessed March 28, 2020.

23 "Vine Stars Are Leaving for Facebook and Other Platforms," WSJ, accessed March 28, 2020.

instead of Vine; the Vine community website shut down in January.[24]

2014

FACEBOOK MESSENGER

In 2014, Facebook released a messaging app. Facebook didn't want to end up like Myspace, so the app needed to keep diversifying its offerings and continue being the most frequently used app.

2016

ByteDance first launched Douyin for the China market in September, 2016. This is the company that brought us TikTok. The TikTok mobile app allows users to create a short videos of themselves, which often feature music in the background, can be sped up, slowed down, or edited with a filter.[25]

2017

TikTok was launched for iOS and Android in markets outside of mainland China.[26]

2018

TikTok became available in the United States after merging with Musical.ly.

---

24   "Twitter Axes Vine Video Service," BBC News, accessed March 28, 2020.
25   "How to Use TikTok: Tips for New Users," Wired, accessed March 28, 2020.
26   "ByteDance," Bytedance.com, accessed March 28, 2020.

2020

WHAT'S NEXT?

Social media platforms are always changing and innovating.

Whenever there's an app or iOS update, I roll my eyes because I have to learn a different layout or strategy, where everything is located, or new features; and this was no different when TikTok became big.

The new and greatest social app of 2020 has been TikTok. The social app has taken off by storm, creating new "influencers" on the platform. When there is a clean slate on new platforms, new stars are born.

Before you know it, sixteen-year-old Charli D'Amelio is Tik-Tok famous. If you aren't familiar with who that is, D'Amelio creates dance videos with trending songs on the platform. D'Amelio's TikTok account, as of August, 2020, has over eighty million followers.[27]

D'Amelio has already signed with a management company and a talent agency, and she has appeared in a Super Bowl commercial for Sabra Hummus—seriously. She's a sixteen-year-old making dance videos. If the world liked my dance videos to Brittany Spears and NSYNC, I'd happily sacrifice my embarrassment for this lifestyle.

We've grown our technology and how we connect with each other tremendously through the last decade, especially

---

27   "Charli D'Amelio Is TikTok's Biggest Star. She Has No Idea Why," The Washington Post, accessed March 28, 2020.

throughout 2000s as whole. Understanding how social media has evolved will help you better understand how the women in this book have utilized these platforms to enhance their products, companies, and brands.

CHAPTER 2

FROM HOLLYWOOD SOCIALITES TO DIGITAL INFLUENCERS

———

As different social media channels surfaced on our screens, so too did Hollywood socialites.

For the first time because of different social media channels, everyday people had access to celebrities like they never had before. Before social media, we would get information through tabloids, long-form blogs, Perez Hilton (insert eye roll here), and other media outlets that exerted more control over what they wanted their audience to see and hear. Now, we have instant access with all different kinds of information straight from celebrities at our fingertips whenever we want.

You might know Paris Hilton from her famous quote "that's hot" or from her popular reality television series, *The Simple Life*, but what you probably don't know is that Paris Hilton is a straight up I.C.O.N.

*Paris helped write the script on how to build a brand through social media and set the precedent for everyone to exist in this internet-driven world.

The modern-day ideas of celebrities, how brands market on social media, the way we think about influence all started with Paris. She has parlayed her media fame into an eponymous brand, which includes nineteen product lines, fifty boutiques worldwide, and a club resort in Manila, Philippines. Her perfume line alone has brought in over three billion dollars in revenue.[28] *Variety* magazine even named her its "Billion Dollar Entrepreneur."[29]

HILTON WAS AHEAD OF HER TIME.
The social media moguls we know and love today follow the same tactics she created years ago. When she was paving the way, there was no agent, publicist, or stylist for her to hire—nothing. When the Hilton sisters moved to New York, Paris was fifteen years old. They quickly started getting invited to parties, so she grew up fast living in a place like New York City. According to the popular documentary *American Meme* produced by Paris, she talks about wanting to create her own identity—away from the family business. She didn't want to be known as the granddaughter of Hilton Hotels.

She talks about the importance of technology in an interview with *Paper Magazine*, saying "I have always been a huge tech

---

28 "Inside Paris Hilton's Multi-Billion Dollar Retail Empire," Daily Mail, accessed March 28, 2020.

29 "'Ditzy Blonde' No More: Paris Hilton Reinvents Herself As A Serious Entrepreneur -- And Crushes It," Forbes, accessed March 28, 2020.

geek and have always been obsessed with technology. Yes, I agree in some way that it has made people more isolated in the fact that people are always on their phones constantly and no longer have many face-to-face or even phone conversations and interactions. But I love it because I have a direct line of communication to all my fans around the world and can connect with them. And as a businesswoman, technology is an amazing marketing tool."[30]

In 2002, Paris met a famous photographer named David LaChapelle. Paris was a huge fan of his work. He is best known for his photography, which often references art history and sometimes conveys social messages. His photographic style has been described as "hyper-real and slyly subversive" and as "kitsch pop surrealism."[31] When they first connected, David asked Paris what her name was. When she replied, he said "You're a star. You're my muse like Andy Warhol had Edith Minturn Sedgwick."

Paris was very young at the time (nineteen years old) and LaChapelle had an idea. He invited her and her sister Nikki (sixteen years old) to have a photo shoot. The Hilton sisters' parents were very strict with them, so they lied and said they were headed off to their cousin's birthday party while LaChapelle and his team flew the sisters out for a night that would follow Paris for the rest of her life. They ended up shooting at a famous motel in Los Angeles, wearing risqué clothing and

---

30 "How Paris Hilton Invented the Social Media Star," PAPER, accessed March 28, 2020.
31 "David LaChapelle: Maximum Exposure," The Guardian, accessed March 28, 2020.

necklaces that said "rich." These photos included half-naked photos of Paris she thought would never been seen.

Days later, LaChapelle called Paris with the news that *Vanity Fair* loved the photos. After those photos were released in the magazine, Paris was known as the crazy socialite-turned-party-girl. From that point on, her world exploded.

She did everything on her own and used the media to her advantage. Her content was so authentic and organic, and it helped her build her empire. Today, everything is more man-ufactured. Women go get styled head-to-toe just to run an errand, to shoot Instagram content, or to show their follow-ers the "look of the day." Paris says, "the press started to call me 'famous for being famous,' which I think is actually an awesome thing; to be able to create something just by being yourself." Some would argue that she was already famous because of her family wealth, but Paris used the media and press to present an extension of who she was to the world.

Just having money doesn't always translate into having a company and massive amounts of success. Read that again.

Take Blake Lively for example. You might remember awhile back Lively tried her hand at the lifestyle game with her web-site *Preserve* in 2014, but Gwyneth Paltrow already domi-nated that market with *Goop*, a website she started in 2008.

Yes, Paltrow already had a running start, but the biggest difference was people had no idea what in the world Lively's website was about. *Goop's* main focus was a lifestyle brand and began as a weekly e-mail newsletter providing new-age advice, such as "eliminating white foods" to "Nourish the Inner Aspect"—content digestible to understand and partake in.[32] Lively's site didn't even last a full year before shutting down. Many claim that it was due to the fact it was unclear what the site was trying to be.

In Lively's own words on the now-defunct site, *Preserve* was "part magazine, part e-commerce hub, part philanthropic endeavor and—above all—a place to showcase the power of imagination, ingenuity, quality, and (simply put) people."[33] Those are a lot of words that don't actually mean anything. When Lively announced that she was shutting down *Preserve,* she said it was because the site was "not making a difference in people's lives, whether superficially or in a meaningful way." In other words, website was a flop.[34]

Celebrity doesn't equal a successful company. There's a tactic and method to building something special that people want to be a part of or buy. Other celebrities like Kim Kardashian, Kylie Jenner, and Gwyneth Paltrow are all examples of women who understood the power of social media and how it could be used as a marketing tool. They've created

32 "Just a Bunch of Goop," BaltimoreSun.com, accessed March 28, 2020.
33 "31 Celebrities Who Tried — and Failed — to Start Their Own Businesses – Insider," Insider, accessed March 28, 2020.
34 "Blake Lively's Preserve: An Obituary," Vanity Fair, accessed March 28, 2020.

companies that reach over millions of people all around the world with products and services no one has created before.

Despite Kim Kardashian's initial rise to fame and success, her sister, Kylie Jenner, is wealthier than most members of the Kardashian/Jenner family.

Jenner is now on *Forbes'* annual world billionaires list and remains the planet's youngest self-made billionaire at twenty-two years old—and yes, I said self-made. Despite a lot of help from her famous family, she didn't inherit a business, she built one.[35] A lot of people would say all you need is to inherit a few hundred million dollars and have access to famous friends and family for it to be possible to make something of yourself. But what people don't understand is that Jenner was worth just five million dollars in 2015, and, fewer than four years later, she'd become the world's first self-made billionaire. If you still don't think she's self-made, try achieving a 19,900.00 percent return on investment in four years and let me know how that goes.[36]

Perhaps Jenner wouldn't have been named the world's youngest billionaire as quickly if she hadn't come from a famous family, but that's not to say she wouldn't have achieved such success in her lifetime. With more than one-hundred-and-seventy-five million followers across all her social platforms—Facebook, Instagram, and Snapchat—social media has been a key to Jenner's success. You might even remember the time

---

35   "Kylie Jenner Is Still The Youngest Self-Made Billionaire In The World," Forbes accessed March 28, 2020.

36   "Kylie Jenner: Is She Really a 'self-Made' Billionaire?" BBC News, accessed March 28, 2020.

when Jenner tweeted that she no longer used Snapchat after an update redesigned the app making it extremely hard to use (I even remember deleting the app because it was so difficult to use). Jenner wiped $1.3 billion off Snap's stock market value; talk about influential.[37]

What Paris Hilton and Kylie Jenner both have in common is, despite their family wealth, they built their own empires from the ground up. Hilton and Jenner are also connected by Kim Kardashian.

Long before anyone even knew who the Kardashians were, Kim Kardashian was Paris Hilton's personal stylist. While working together, they became very close. Kardashian even says on an episode of *Keeping Up With The Kardashians*, "Paris literally gave me a career."[38] I guess Kardashian's early career with Hilton paid off since a thing or two she'd learned from the heiress trickled into the rest of the Kardashian/Jenner clan.

Of course, it doesn't hurt to have a cash pile in the closet in case you make a mistake, but building a brand takes work—hard work. What they also have in common is creating something that their communities can relate to. Hilton captured the media's attention to advertise her ventures like her perfume or book deals and used that to her advantage during a time where social media had not taken off yet. Jenner's community was interested in something different: her lips.

37 Ibid.
38 "Kim Kardashian Says Paris Hilton 'gave Me a Career' as She Reunites with Old Friend," Mail Online, accessed August 22, 2020.

Jenner is known for her ever-changing lips. She's famous for using clever lip makeup tricks, such as over-lining the lips and filling them in with a natural-looking matte base. Some mocked her look, and media surrounding her lips got so crazy that a viral (and painful) challenge to plump their own lips sparked on social media. Interest can be weird sometimes. Because women wanted to get this same look, the products Jenner was rumored to use sold out at MAC Cosmetics outlets across the world. This is when the business idea "sparked" for Jenner. She would build an empire around what she is known for: makeup advice and products for your lips.

Jenner knew her community of fans on Instagram and Snapchat spent months trialing three shades of nude lip liner and matte lip cream combos based on her look. When Jenner launched her first shades, the lip kits sold out in less than a minute and crashed the website. This trend became normal for Jenner. Jenner's brand has kept people hooked by maintaining marketing tactics that other beauty brands have picked up on, such as using countdowns to reveal products on social media, selling them on a limited release, and often collaborating with famous people—in Jenner's case her siblings—making you feel like you had to have this lip kit before it was too late.

I'll even admit, I have F.O.M.O. (fear of missing out) on her lip kits. Back in 2016, I was sitting in my office when I lived in Washington, D.C. working for a start-up social media agency. I remember telling all my coworkers at 3:00 p.m. EST, Jenner was releasing her lip kits, and we all had to be online to see if anyone could get through checkout to purchase one of the lip kits. Every time I tried to get a lip kit in the past, they were literally sold out within five minutes. That was beyond anything I have ever done before: making sure I get a product made by an eighteen-year-old during my workday. This was crazy.

Kylie Cosmetic's is not alone; brands such as Huda Beauty and Anastasia Beverly Hills have soared in popularity in recent years. YouTube endorsements in particular have the power to make a product a "must have." It cannot be said enough how significant influencer and online marketing are. Jenner changed and took a different approach within an industry she believed had gone stale in its marketing efforts in the past.

We're no longer going to the beauty counter at Nordstrom to get opinions on skin care or makeup; it's more authentic getting advice from someone you know, trust, and care about as opposed to a faceless corporation. These celebrities have taken a look at what they've been known for and turned that into a business.

CHAPTER 3

THE RISE OF INFLUENCER MARKETING

Most people don't know this, but the world "influencer" was officially added to the English dictionary in 2019.[39] By now, influencer marketing is far from a new concept to most. Nowadays, we're often influenced from experiences with our friends and family or look to aspirational figures for inspiration on what to buy.

One of the first recorded influencer collaborations dates back all the way to the 1760s, when a potter by the name of Wedgewood made a tea set for the queen of England.[40] Since monarchy was equivalent modern-day influencers, his forward-thinking decision to market his brand as royal-approved afforded it the luxury status the brand still has today.

---

39 "[Timeline] A Brief History of Influencers," Social Media Today, accessed August 22, 2020.

40 Ibid.

In recent years, social media has given us the platform to share recommendations from others from all over the world. This quick evolution of influencer marketing has exploded into the fast-growing, billion-dollar industry we know today. Jim Tobin, the President and Founder of Carusele, an influencer agency says, "The maturation of influencer marketing in many ways mirrors how social media marketing grew from 2007 – 2012. It moved from interesting and buzzworthy to a driver of business results and, as it did so, the amount of marketing dollars invested grew by billions."[41]

Whether or not you support the influencer world (being an influencer or using influencers for your brand), we can all agree that they created a completely new category that's shaped the way we connect, buy, and engage on social media. Even the Federal Trade Commission had to create rules around advertising to consumers and how influencers have to disclose certain information to their followers. For a while now, the FTC has required influencers to disclose sponsored posts, but the guidelines seem to have had little effect.

In one recent case, a Lord & Taylor campaign paid fifty social media influencers to post about a dress on Instagram but didn't require them to disclose that the posts were sponsored. The FTC charged Lord & Taylor with deceiving the public, settling the case by prohibiting the company from "misrepresenting that paid ads are from an independent source," but didn't levy a monetary fine.[42] With the rapid growth of influ-

41   "Influencer Marketing Predictions for 2020 - Top Industry Experts Weigh In," Influencer Marketing Hub, accessed August 22, 2020.
42   "Lord & Taylor Settles FTC Charges It Deceived Consumers Through Paid Article in an Online Fashion Magazine and Paid Instagram Posts

encer marketing, the FTC had to put regulations in place to prohibit unfair or deceptive advertising on any medium. So many people and brands have easy access to create accounts and try to become influencers, advertising any product or message they want to. Some influencers have advantages if they were working with an influencer agency or agent. Most companies are well up to speed on the current regulations and guidelines.

Not only are rules and regulations being put in place for this new industry, marketing managers for brands are looking for methods to grow their brand's influencer marketing. Influencer marketing budgets are increasing month after month on average by sixty-seven percent.[43]

Instagram has seen an explosion of use over the last few years. The idea that its users post ninety-five million photos and videos, and "like" over four billion posts every day is mind boggling.[44] Instagram has played a huge role in helping micro-influencers and small businesses expand their audience to a broader one, while also helping increase sales and followers.

Influencer marketing would still exist without digital, but it would look different. Because we're able to communicate across the world with anyone through our phones, including

by 50 'Fashion Influencers,'" Federal Trade Commission, accessed August 22, 2020.

43 "37 Instagram Statistics That Matter to Marketers in 2020." Social Media Marketing & Management Dashboard, accessed August 22, 2020.

44 Ibid.

via social media, brands and influencers are able to extend their reach beyond the front steps of their doors.

Rising with influencer marketing is the perception of getting easy money by trying to become a famous social media influencer. With influencers earning well over five thousand dollars per post, everyone wants in. But, because of the rapid growth of this industry and everyone wanting to cash in, there's an oversaturation that points to a negative side.

Did the rise of social platforms like Instagram give early adopters the opportunity to build huge, loyal followings early on? Did they have an advantage over others who tried to become "insta-famous" later on? I'm still seeing friends and family turn hobbies into Instagram businesses—literally anyone can create a small business using Instagram—but how do you know if you have what it takes to end up with millions of followers? Has it become too much with everyone thinking they can turn their personal brand into a business? So many people have tried their hand at growing a social media following to the point where a luxury boutique hotel in Ireland banned all YouTube and Instagram stars after getting a request to stay at the hotel in exchange for exposure.[45]

So the real question is, can everyone that attempts Insta-fame succeed?

---

45   "The Rise and Fall of the Social Media Influencer," Marketing Insider Group, accessed August 22, 2020.

You have to have something that is different about what you bring to the table—something that sets you apart. What is your story, and why are you unique? Not everyone has the skill set to expand on their uniqueness to become successful using digital. Truth be told, some are just simply better at influencing than others.

Take Serena F*cking Kerrigan. If you've heard of her, you know she has branded herself as the Queen of Confidence. Now, I know she isn't in the fashion or beauty industries, but I'm talking about her because she paints you a picture of taking a chance on yourself using social media and why influencer marketing is more than just "being an influencer."

Kerrigan left her role at Refinery29 where she was over-seeing short-firm digital content and long-form narratives across their social media platforms. She wanted to focus on building her own empire, SFK, the Queen of Confidence. During her time at Refinery29, she talked all about con-fidence and centered her content around this subject. The more she talked about it, the more her vision came to life. She realized this could be turned into a brand and it was time to focus on it.

Once she left her day job, Kerrigan went full speed ahead on her project. You can find Kerrigan often posting stories about female empowerment, how to love yourself, and giving women confidence they need to achieve anything they put their minds to. You might be thinking to yourself, "well, a lot of women do this on social media," but she wasn't just an influencer who was posting what she ate or wore. She knew she had to stand out from the rest. So, she changed the digital dating landscape and produced a first reality show entirely on Instagram Live: *Let's Fucking Date.*[46]

It's brilliant because what do you do during COVID-19 when you can't date, or see people? Build a real-time dating show everyone has access to watch. No editing plus no script equals pure enjoyment.

Each week, Kerrigan goes on a set-up, blind date while thousands of fans and friends watch in real time. It goes down in the comment section as fans and friends can share their thoughts and opinions during the live dating show. Even Jennifer Lopez's hairdresser has joined to watch. Big media names, *The Today Show*, *CBNC* and more, have also picked up likes of the show.[47]

It's not just about becoming an influencer and the persona Kerrigan created, there's more to it than that. She's both building a brand and creating a business. Her timing, uniqueness, and creativity are why she's been successful. Kerrigan is bringing something to the table no one has done yet, and in doing so, she set herself apart. She's able to influence because:

1. She knows her audience and tailors her content, female empowerment, to reach the right people.
2. She sets herself apart with her live dating show through Instagram—the first of its kind to not require a production crew.

---

46 "Serena Kerrigan," Serena Kerrigan, Accessed August 22, 2020.
47 Ibid.

3. She built a product tied to her dating show and created a business, a "card game" to play and help you conquer the world of dating, expanding the definition of "influencer."

Because she knows her audience and has a clear path of what to put out there on her social media platforms, she's able to effectively influence her community through her channel with her content and her products.

As you've read, some are better at influencing others through social media because they know their audience and what their audience wants to see. Each influencer and celebrity tailor their content to their platforms and gain increased trust in their communities—a quality attractive to brands and future partnerships. It has increased the return on investment of brands because of targeted exposure. It's becoming more popular to partner with an influencer to position your credibility, identity, and brand image.

Influencer marketing is working, and more people are trying to become famous by expanding their own personal brands through digital and creating a sustainable living. It's important to understand how influencer marketing works. Some of the brands these women built tapped into this market and created their own influencer campaigns. The ability to expand personal brand to reach new fans and consumers speaks to how powerful a tool influencer marketing is to use for brand visibility.

Relevant influencers and branded digital content continue to become one of the most powerful tools available to marketers as well as entrepreneurs.

CHAPTER 4

BRICK-AND-MORTAR TO DIGITAL STOREFRONTS

───

I remember a time when I used to go to the mall and shop around with my girlfriends. I would tell my parents that I was going to the mall with friends, but secretly, I would go on dates with my boyfriend. It's where we went back then as a "cool" hang out spot. Besides going to the mall as a fun activity, I went to the mall to shop for clothes, buy music, and grab lunch, and I'd end up spending hours there. Now, I sit on my couch while watching *Bravo* and online shopping—not just for clothes but for literally everything from household items to grocery shopping. You can now buy everything online, and I mean everything. Slowly, more and more brick-and-mortar stores are turning their store fronts into digital ones.

More than eight-hundred thousand shoppers use *Instagram* every month simply by scrolling through their news feed or getting served an ad for something they never thought they needed until then.[48] Celebrities and influencers are now able to create digital storefronts through their social pages, allowing users to purchase anything with a click of a button. The evolution of the digital world and how it's changed the way we're influenced, how we shop, how we buy, whose opinions we value and get information from, has changed the game of how we shop. The access we have within our pockets has made shopping as easy as the swipe of a finger.

INSTANT COMMUNICATION

Being able to create an online community to get one-to-one feedback on products is a gold mine. So many influencers have created a strong community of followers and been able to create products based on community feedback. Many influencers will hold their design meetings online and ask their followers to give feedback on what they like better. Including their followers in part of the journey makes them feel like they are involved and invested in the success of this product.

We're also seeing private messaging emerge in the social media world. It's crazy to think consumers are able to message influencers or their favorite social media celebrities and have one-on-one conversations about products or lifestyle. One-on-one messaging and private chat groups are on fire right now. Facebook messenger has nine-hundred million global users, and studies have shown that teenagers now spend more time on messaging apps than they do on actual

---

48 "Instagram Shopping: Does It Work? (It Does For These Brands)," The BigCommerce Blog, accessed March 28, 2020.

social networks.[49] If you're building a product for teens, you should put potential efforts on content creation involving interactions between users. This is why knowing your audience is very beneficial.

For example, Snapchat reaches more thirteen to thirty-four-year-old's in the US than Facebook or Instagram, and the one-hundred million users Snapchat reaches in the US is more users than Twitter and TikTok combined.[50] If your audience falls in that range, you should consider shifting your content to these platforms. This is where your audience can have that instant communication with you as a brand or an influencer.

Snapchat reminded us that over thirty times per day, one-hundred-and-thirty-five million people create augmented reality (AR) with its camera daily, and one million people interact with it.[51] A big announcement was SnapML.[52] This allows developers to bring their own machine learning models into the Snap Lens Studio, highlighting language learning and commerce in early use cases. Snapchat also announced 3D face meshing, skeleton tracking, and AR material programming. Importantly, Snapchat announced products built

49 "9 Ways Digital Has Changed Business Forever," Digital Marketing Institute, accessed March 28, 2020.
50 "Average Time Spent Daily on Social Media (Latest 2020 Data)," BroadbandSearch.net, accessed March 28, 2020.
51 "Snap Says 170 Million Use Its Augmented Reality Tools Daily," Bloomberg.com, accessed August 22, 2020.
52 "Snapchat Boosts Its AR Platform with Voice Search, Local Lenses and SnapML," TechCrunch, accessed August 22, 2020.

in the Snap Lens Studio work in all of Snapchat's software development kits, including its AR glasses, Spectacles.[53]

Technology's advancement on these social platforms allows you to create more customized content tailored to your brand, like QUAY, for example. When I was searching for blue light glasses, I found that their website offers virtual try-on's, allowing me to ensure I'd like them and they'd fit my face and personality. Being able to see a product on your body before you purchase, without physically wearing the product, shows us how far a user's shopping experience has come on these channels.

CONTENT, CONTENT, CONTENT

Today, in 2020, some 3.8 million people use social media, which is more than half the world's population.[54] That's millions of pieces of content being shared around the world. We're able to create our own story using the content we want. Before social media, the media (if you were starting to get noticed) controlled your story, just like they did with Paris Hilton. She created a brand based off of what the media was selling. Now, everyone can create content tailored to who they are, too. People have the opportunity to discover new influencers or brands they wouldn't have had access to before without social media.

---

53 "Spectacles by Snap Inc. • Capture Your World in 3D," Spectacles.com, accessed August 22, 2020.

54 "Digital 2020: 3.8 Billion People Use Social Media - We Are Social," We Are Social, accessed March 28, 2020.

Just like when I use to go to the mall, I love to shop around and see what's new now through digital. With Facebook and Instagram's algorithms, the platforms are able to show you content you engage with the most, keeping you interested in the things you love.

SHOW ME THE NUMBERS

With modern technology offering insight and statistics on social platforms, influencers and brands now gain tremendous amounts of knowledge about the preferences, behaviors, and interests of their community members and fans. However, you need to know how, where, and when to use that data. Some of the best ways to utilize this insight is knowing which metrics are most important to the success of your brand. The key to get a positive impact from analyzing your data is knowing what your followers want to get from your content and comparing to what you're putting out there. This means being very specific about what your business objectives and goals are and building that into how the data is measured and how it impacts your brand as a whole.

Knowing which channels are going to pay off is another key. There are so many social channels out there, so focusing on the channels your community will engage with in a meaningful way is beneficial. If you're personally using Twitter as your platform but are talking about skin care, you probably need to look into putting in more advertisement dollars and shifting your content to Instagram. There, you'll be talking to the right audience and start to see better results.

Back in the day, we could put up a billboard sign to advertise our businesses. Unfortunately, we'd have no idea who saw the billboard, let alone which age group was passing by it most. Were people pulling over to read the sign and learn more? Probably not! Having the backend filled with insights on platforms like Facebook, Instagram, LinkedIn, etc. has helped so many influencers and brands know their audiences' wants and customize their content to better suit this better-defined market.

Studying these insights each week to pivot your social media behavior can help the performance of your business, tremendously. Some social media platforms have insights that others don't have. For example, Facebook and Instagram provide you with how many people your account reached, content interaction data, total follower count with demographics, location, age, and more. Insights like this can help you shift your brand where it needs to be. This is why becoming familiar with your data is so important.

When you know your numbers and you're able to know who you're creating products and content for, your content becomes more personalized to your audience. You have less than five seconds to capture someone's attention, so your content should scream who you are without someone having to look at your profile name and picture.

TRANSPARENCY

Let's be real; faking it until you make it only works so far. You need real transparency. We've seen more and more influencers expose their lives deeper—sharing more intimate moments with their community. In today's digital world, there are lots of fakes: people who just simply don't have what it takes to rise to the top. In order to build loyalty, influencers and brands need to be transparent and demonstrate their personality and the company's ethos online. This is particularly relevant when it comes to beauty products with consumers wanting to know exactly what's in their skin care or makeup.

Gwyneth Paltrow stressed how vital it was that her line of beauty products—including a face cleanser, eye cream, and moisturizer—was all-natural.[55] "The idea that you're exercising and trying to eat well and then slathering yourself with chemicals, parabens, and silicones—it's not great."[56] A few months later, she went on *The Tonight Show* to promote her line.[57] She and host Jimmy Fallon dipped McDonald's French fries into a pot of her moisturizer and ate them, presumably to show how pure her product was—talk about transparency!

Social media and video outlets like YouTube have enabled "regular" people to become incredibility influential. Brands no longer need to hire celebrities or to call the media for photographs.

Now, ordinary people with no credentials other than a large number of followers on social media have the ability

55 "Gwyneth Paltrow Split with Condé Nast over Fact-Checking," Vox, accessed March 28, 2020.

56 "Gwyneth Paltrow Introduces Goop by Juice Beauty Skin Care," Vogue, accessed March 28, 2020.

57 "Gwyneth Paltrow and Jimmy Eat Her Goop Skincare Line," YouTube, accessed March 28, 2020.

to influence those simply by endorsing a certain product or even creating a product.

Take Chiara Ferragni, the founder of *The Blonde Salad* website. Ferragni took her fashion blog and turned it into a global retail business. Born as a fashion blogger, Ferragni first became an influencer then a successful entrepreneur. She is also a stylist; she created and signed several fashion collections. In 2015, the turnover of her company was ten million dollars; today her company has twenty employees and she runs her own e-commerce store. With over seventeen million followers on Instagram, she is a fashion icon. And to make her even more perfect, her husband is an Italian superstar rapper who also has a huge following on Instagram, making their combined twenty-five followers million equal to the population of Australia.[58]

Ferragni, while living in Milan, started taking photos outside fashion shows and began her blog, *The Blonde Salad*, discussing her takes on fashion. "It was all about mixing it up, just like you would a salad," she said, playing on the cliché of the dumb blonde. As her fame grew fast to make a living, she quit studying at Bocconi University just three exams short of graduation. By this time, her blog had reached more than one million unique visitors and boasted twelve million views per month.

With her blog reaching so many people, Ferragni saw the potential to grow her personal brand into a fashion and

---

58 "Why Is Chiara Ferragni Famous?" A Day in the Life, accessed March 28, 2020.

business icon. She moved to Los Angeles in 2013 to expand her business, and, after learning English and losing her Italian accent (because she wanted to internationalize herself), *Forbes* named her "30 under 30" on their list of power brokers. *Spanish Vogue* put her on its cover. Even Harvard Business School used her as a case-study in how to monetize the dual streams of a blog and a personal brand as a business. She did all of this within three years—talk about a woman on the move.[59]

One of the biggest reasons Ferragni was successful and achieved so much is her <u>transparency</u>.

She had a genuine look and style about her, which she reflected in her blog. On the web, she talked about her personal life: traveling between Milan and Cremona, university lessons, and, of course, shopping. She is not only up front and honest about who she is and her style, but she responds to her fans with advice, emojis, and gratitude for being a fan. She's completely transparent in her messaging back to her fans, making her connections to her fans personal. She's able to create lifelong fans who stick around not only because of the styles she puts together or the looks she creates, but because she's one of the first women to create a new industry and is a leading lady paving a path for future influencers to follow. Sabina Belli, chief executive of jewelry

---

59 "Chiara Ferragni — the Italian Influencer Who Built a Global Brand," FinancialTimes, accessed March 28, 2020.

brand Pomellato, used Ferragni for an advertising campaign, and she said Ferragni's vision and drive to become the most powerful fashion influencer in the world is an "admirable feat" for any entrepreneur. "Chiara speaks directly to the digital generation," she adds.[60]

POP-UP SHOPS

We're starting to see a new business model emerge, especially in the apparel and beauty sector. More and more brands are using social media to reach their fans and communities by creating unique experiences. Influencers partnering with brands, or even brands alone, are opening standalone 'pop-up' stores, creating a new experience for their consumers. Kylie Jenner created a one-of-a-kind experience with her pop-up store in the Westfield Topanga Mall in Los Angeles. If you follow Jenner on Snapchat, you would have seen the hundreds of dedicated fans that lined up the night before at nine o'clock, waiting for the store to open at ten o'clock the next morning.

Inside the store, Jenner and her team created an entire wall, top to bottom, of *every* lip kit she'd ever made.[61] To put that in perspective, she's made around one hundred different types of lip kits available for purchase. Aside from her cosmetics, you could also buy socks, underwear, phone cases, and more in the pop-up shop. She extended her world to her fans, allowing them to buy into an experience and offering them a wide range of products not only in the beauty

60   Ibid.

61   "Kylie Jenner Builds A Crazy Wall of Lip Kits for Pop-Up Shop." YouTube, accessed March 28, 2020.

department. In doing so, she further expanded her brand and empire.

While online retail is growing and the instant access to it always in our pocket, there remains significant opportunities for both online and in-store retailers to customize offerings to better align with consumer expectations. There are many opportunities to increase sales by bringing consumers back in-store with limited-time experiences like the pop-up store. It creates a sense of urgency to visit before it disappears and is a great way to poll your target customers offline, selling new products alongside your usual inventory and getting customer feedback on the spot. Influencers partnering with brands or standalone brands can benefit from face-to-face interaction. It goes back to that instant connection, but it makes the connection more personal. For example, even having the founder show up to the opening to get customer feedback and give immediate answers to questions or concerns is powerful.

Consumers are more inclined to browse online than they are to get in their cars, drive to a store, and walk around. Being able to access things such as shopping websites and blogs to browse the latest trends doesn't mean retail shopping is dying. Like we saw with Jenner and her pop-up shop with the massive lip kit wall or Glossier transforming their pop-up shop into a full blown experience as if you're in the grand canyon (more on this later), we've become needy as consumers and want to experience something personal from a brand or influencer. This makes pop-up shops trendy and popular to weave into your marketing plans.

Before jumping into your car in search of the perfect space for your own pop-up store, pump the breaks. While it can be dreamy to think about a cool space to design YOU would absolutely love and want to shop at, there's a lot more work to be done before you start to invest in retail landscape, even if you're only renting it for a couple of months. A lot of success stories in this book follow a similar process I like to call the 4S process, which we'll talk about throughout this book.

CHAPTER 5

AN INTRODUCTION TO THE 4S PROCESS

———

Throughout my career, I've read so many stories of women who have built products I use in my everyday life and couldn't imagine living without. As you already know, I'm a sucker for trying new products and love reporting back to friends about my experience. After reading countless interviews on "how they grow so fast" or "what the secret is to their success," I noticed how celebrities and influencers have been able to take their own personal brands and turn that into a business, specifically through digital.

While capturing this research, these women had built empires within the beauty and fashion space, making new and innovative ways to market on social media, and I wanted to know how they did it. Every one of them had a different angle yet used this same formula to transform their brand into a full-time business.

I LIKE TO CALL IT THE 4S PROCESS, WHICH INCLUDES:
- **Spark** - What sparked the idea?
- **Social Media** - How did these women leverage social media to build a community?
- **Secret Sauce** - What was their secret sauce? What made them different enough to stand out in a sea of wannabes?
- **Success** - How did they grow their brand to gain the level of success they had?

Now, I'm not saying this process couldn't apply to other industries like travel, fitness or health, but this specifically applies to the fashion and beauty space where I saw these common themes. The types of women and stories I connect this process to all relate back to the beauty and fashion industries.

THE SPARK - FINDING YOUR UNIQUE VOICE

For each successful person, there was an event or moment that sparked the idea. It could be anyone, from a celebrity who was already known for something or an influencer who had built their following through a trend that hadn't existed yet. For Huda Kattan, she never wanted to be a CEO of a company, but that all changed when her sister, Mona, convinced her to go to school to study makeup; it had always been a passion of hers. Kattan was struggling to find direction in her life. She had a degree in finance but didn't have the passion to pursue a career in it, so she went to beauty school. [62]

---

62 "How Huda Kattan Built a Multi-Million-Dollar Beauty Brand from a Blog," Fast Company, accessed March 28, 2020.

In 2010, two years after Kattan and husband Christopher Goncalo moved to Dubai, she started her blog titled *Huda Beauty*, which developed a considerable presence on social media and YouTube. Kattan states "The blog had become this marketing tool that had allowed me to get into this new wave. When I started blogging, all the makeup artists around me were like, "you're crazy—you're giving out free advice."[63] Sharing that advice paid off because by sharing beauty tips and tricks with her community, she built a loyal fan base that couldn't wait until Kattan dropped her own beauty product: false eyelashes.

Kattan had started creating products of her own for fun, including false eyelashes, which her sister encouraged her to start selling. With a loan from her sister, Kattan launched her lashes in 2013, quickly becoming a booming success. They sold out across Sephora Dubai and made waves stateside when Kim Kardashian wore a pair. *Forbes* later named her one of the richest self-made women.

I had never owned eyelashes in my life until a couple of years ago. Now, for any big event that I have coming up, I have to wear false eyelashes. But why have we all started adding this into our beauty routine? It's because we're influenced, now, by the people who we follow on social media. Kattan's beauty blog sparked her idea to create a new beauty product that wasn't on people's radar, until now.

---

63   "How I Became a Makeup Mogul: Beauty Influencer Huda Kattan Talks about Business, Life," USA TODAY, accessed March 28, 2020.

SOCIAL MEDIA - GROWING YOUR UNIQUE VOICE, LEVERAGE DIGITAL CONNECTION

In 2018, Instagram reached one billion users and became an advertising powerhouse.[64] During this time, Google received sixty-one thousand search queries for "influencer marketing" a month.[65] Instagram was centered on storytelling, and we all know people love a good story. Storytelling is simply part of human nature. And from a business perspective, telling an interesting story is a great way to create an emotional connection with your community and fan base.

This is where a lot of people start. They say write "what you know," and a lot of the stories about women in this book start with blogs. When Instagram launched, blogs became an extension of that. Shorter-form content that had a visual appeal led to spending hours on end going down an information rabbit hole. This was the year users, bloggers, and brands found a new way to communicate and share with their communities. Some of the most successful brands and influencers leveraged social media to grow their own business. Influencers and celebrities could now link their blogs to their profile and showcase longer forms of content. Social media gained an extension and a crucial tool to help advertise and promote brands.

Social media has also been a great tool to get validation. You can get instant feedback from your community on which products they want to see when you're creating something,

---

64 "Ultimate Guide to Instagram For Fashion: Content, Analytics, Influencers, & More!" Later Blog, accessed March 28, 2020.

65 "Influencer Marketing: State of the Social Media Influencer Market in 2020 - Business Insider," Business Insider, accessed March 28, 2020.

using their takes to guide where the product is headed. Emily Weiss, the founder and CEO of *Glossier*, does an amazing job at this. For example, she created a Slack channel for customers to converse about what they liked and didn't like about the products. Weiss has explained in many interviews how she has based current products (and products not yet on the market) off of customer feedback. Before turning your idea into a business, be sure you have validation. Using your community as a research group is the best form of free marketing there is, and it will help grow your audience even more.

SECRET SAUCE: FINDING YOUR UNIQUE BRAND

In 2019, the first influencers were given the power to sell directly through Instagram shoppable tags, making it even easier for people to shop through Instagram. Remember, the word 'influencer' was officially added to the English dictionary in this year.

Rihanna was first discovered by American record producer Evan Rogers in Barbados in 2003, securing a contact with Def Jam Recordings, the chairman of which was Jay-Z. Her career took off quickly, achieving ever rising levels of success in her music career. You know her from her worldwide stardom in the early twenty-first century, specifically for her distinctive and versatile voice and her fashionable appearance.

Besides her music career, Rihanna found a way to create a unique brand in the beauty industry called Fenty. Rihanna was inspired to create Fenty Beauty after years and years of experimenting with some of the best beauty products in the industry and still seeing a huge void in the industry for products that performed across all skin types and tones.[66] Even though some would say it was easier for Rihanna to grow a beauty brand with the hefty following she had from her music career, as we talked about earlier, just because you're a celebrity doesn't mean a product is going to be successful. The secret to Rihanna's success was tapping into a wide range of hard-to-match skin tones no one else had been able to do successfully.

Rihanna's beauty brand was named one of the best inventions of 2017.[67] Rihanna was appraised by *Time Magazine* for her beauty products being of high quality with an emphasis on inclusivity. To put this in more context, one of Rihanna's best-selling products, "Gloss Bomb," a universally flattering lip gloss, is sold every three minutes. Overnight, she set a new tone for diversity within the beauty industry, laying down the work to other major brands with forty shades of foundation for "every woman." It's more important than ever when creating products or creating your own personal brand to remember to be inclusive of all people who could potentially purchase a product from you or are following your social channels.

SUCCESS - HOW DID YOU BECOME SUCCESSFUL

The influencer industry will be worth five to ten billion dollars by 2020. Why? Because while every social platform attracts influencers to some degree, Instagram is the gold standard for the group. Nearly four in five (79 percent) brands tap into

---

66   "Fenty Beauty by Rihanna | About | Fenty Beauty." Fenty Beauty, accessed March 28, 2020.

67   "Why It's Rihanna's World." Grazia, accessed March 28, 2020.

Instagram for influencer campaigns, compared to Facebook or YouTube (36 percent), per Influencer Marketing Hub.[68]

A lot of these women's success has come from this main platform, Instagram. For all the fashion lovers out there, you have definitely heard of Julie Sarinana, also known as Sincerely Jules. Sarinana started her blog in 2009 wanting to inspire the world and is now known as one of the top "OG" influencers. In the beginning, blogging was just a hobby for Sarinana. She started building her brand when the blogging craze was just getting started back in 2009. Her success grew out of her love for fashion and creative expression. Today, Sarinana has over five million followers on Instagram.[69]

Sarinana attributes her success to staying true to herself. She says in an interview with *InStyle*, "I know it's very easy to step away from that path, because you're caught up in meeting so many people and you get invited to places, and the money, and this and that. But as long as your stay focused, and you stay grounded and you surround yourself with grounded people, family, and friends, I think that what your goal is, you can reach it."[70]

Although, that's easier said than done; it's hard to filter out the noise and remain focused when the influencer space has become oversaturated and competitive, especially in the

---

68   "Influencer Marketing: State of the Social Media Influencer Market in 2020 - Business Insider," Business Insider, accessed March 28, 2020.

69   "How 'Sincerely Jules' Parlayed Her 5.5M Instagram Followers Into Billabong's Most Successful Collab," Forbes, accessed March 28, 2020.

70   "Style Influencer Sincerely Jules on the Biggest Splurge Item in Her Closet," InStyle.com, accessed March 28, 2020.

fashion and beauty industries today. Sarinana explains in an interview with *Forbes* she has always listened to her heart and gut; doing so helped her grow and achieve the level of success she has today. While staying true to herself, she shares inspirational photos and creates content on her Instagram feed rather than speaking to the camera on the story feature, which doesn't feel authentic to her as a naturally shy person.

Instagram stories are huge for influencers and brands, making this tool a way for influencers to connect on a deeper level with their fans. Sarinana has taken a different approach to her content creation, and it's paid off. Her account is a top destination for those seeking style inspiration. In many interviews, she says over and over that being consistent and truly following your heart contributes to so much of her success.

I've talked about some women who built an empire in the beauty and fashion world and about how we've changed our digital landscape to use social media as a tool to build a business, to become an entrepreneur, and how everything is on our phones, giving us endless access.

Now let's dive deeper into stories about the women I like to call my mentors—the ones that took a chance, ripped up every rule book, and created a different path represented by the 4s process and are the next generation of influencers, entrepreneurs, and all-around BOSSES.

PART 2

THE 4S PROCESS

CHAPTER 6

THE SPARK – FINDING YOUR UNIQUE VOICE | THE PAT MCGRATH STORY

"With persistence, hard work and a whole lot of fantasy, anything is possible"

-PAT MCGRATH

Wouldn't it be great to have every idea we come up with in our heads be a success? I know; I wish it was that easy. I've struggled for years on what ideas to pursue, how to make my ideas spark with a community of people, and how to flip that into a business. What I've learned throughout my twenties is sometimes you find your unique voice through your experiences. A lot of the failures I've read about, including the time I tried to become an influencer myself, never started with "why." Why am I starting this blog? Why do people need to hear this? Why do people need this product? What important message do I have to say that others will follow behind?

Most of the time, we want to start something based on something we are passionate about (of course, no one would start something they aren't passionate about), but we have to look beyond that. Sometimes that unique voice has been in front of us all along, but hasn't been discovered yet.

Makeup is having a major moment on social media. The makeup-obsessed (including me) are taking over social media and using it as a platform to experiment and express themselves with as many selfies as one can post before everyone starts to unfollow you, and so are brands and influencers, making a splash in the money pool with cosmetic lines for consumers to experiment with.

If you're obsessed with sequins like me, then I'm sure you've heard of Pat McGrath. Sequins are a reoccurring element in many of her looks, but McGrath is known for her unique, adventurous, and innovative makeup techniques.[71] She has a talent for using bold hues and material experimentation ranging from feathers to ornaments.[72] Despite having no formal training, McGrath has become one of the most influential and respected makeup artists in the fashion industry.

Not every high-profile artist has successfully enhanced their experience and industry standing with a profitable cosmetics line. What made McGrath have so much success was a

---

71   "Pat McGrath Is Part of the BoF 500," The Business of Fashion, accessed August 1, 2020.
72   Ibid.

combination of star power, great product and packaging, and the smart use of social media to help validate her business. She is fashion's most-requested artist, directing the beauty looks for eighty fashion shows per year, many of whom you might be familiar with: Dolce & Gabbana, Giorgio Armani, and Gucci to name a few.[73]

Growing up in London, McGrath and her mother, Jean, used to go makeup shopping when she was six years old. Fashion became a huge inspiration for her, stimulating her creative approach to makeup. Much of McGrath's inspiration comes from making the natural skin salient. This can be seen in her own makeup line, which focuses on luminous skin. McGrath attributed a lot of her creativity to her mother.

McGrath told Sarah Mower of *Vogue* in 2007, "She trained me, basically, to do the shows, right there... look at the pattern, check the fabrics, look for the makeup, and begin." McGrath explains that her mother was obsessed with makeup. She says, "She would stand in front of the TV, and we'd have to guess what she'd done differently with her eyes. I'd think: 'Get out of my way!' But she wouldn't move until I'd told her."[74]

McGrath and her mother would analyze makeup looks of old Hollywood film stars, identifying which had inspired fashion designers that season. This led to Jean encouraging McGrath to be creative with makeup, mixing pigments from starch to get exactly the right color and adding heat to the skin with her fingertips give a healthier glow and soften the

73   "How Pat McGrath Built a Sell-out Beauty Brand for the Instagram Age," Vogue.It, accessed August 1, 2020.

74   Ibid.

look of foundation. McGrath explains, "She always put on a full face of makeup then got in the bath to get the dewy finish. It was next level, but this is where I got my makeup tips from—at seven years old!"[75]

McGrath completed an art foundation course at Northampton College. She had planned to continue and undertake a fashion degree, but she abandoned this when she met stylist Kim Bowen, who invited her along to watch her work on shoots for *The Face* and *i-D*.

Her Breakthrough Came in the Early 1990s.

McGrath received a phone call asking her to go on tour in Japan with Caron Wheeler from Soul II Soul, who's makeup she'd done one afternoon three years previously as a favor for a friend.

"I left my job and went to Japan for three months, scared to death. I cried all the way there because I'd never been on a plane before and I was terrified," she told The Observer in 2008.[76]

This led to working with Edward Enninful, then fashion director of *i-D* magazine, on shoots for the youth magazine, working fluidly with her hands (which she refers to as

---

75 Ibid.
76 "Pat McGrath Labs Becomes Selfridges Biggest-Selling Beauty Line," The Guardian, accessed August 1, 2020.

brushes) and using her keen eye for bold hues. McGrath has also developed a reputation for material experimentation, often attaching things like petals, feathers, pearls, and other ornaments to models.

Back in 2015 during the Prada runway show, McGrath gave us a first glimpse into a malleable gold metal foil pigment used on the models' lips. And for those that couldn't be there, we saw the show on our digital phones. Needless to say, her makeup stole the show, and an obsession began.

Quickly afterwards, McGrath and her team transformed many stylists, editors, and street style stars using the now-famous metal. This spread like wildfire on social media, creating a spark for McGrath's career. This spark would shape her future, leading to McGrath making millions.

Soon after, McGrath announced she would be launching her gold metal lip product to market, and the countdown began. The lab could only supply one thousand kits, all of which sold out in minutes. In an interview with *The Guardian*, McGrath says "Once it became clear to me that social media would allow me direct, one-on-one dialogue with my customer, plus the opportunity to release compelling content and iconic imagery four times a day, I knew the time was right for Labs."[77]

McGrath's influence on the beauty and fashion industry wasn't just about the innovative makeup techniques she used or the products she made. Her unique voice shined a light on

---

77 Ibid.

an industry as a whole when it comes to diversity, an issue in both fields she experienced firsthand as a young Black girl. She grew up with a limited range of shades for her skin tone. As a result, she consciously worked to change that with her work on runways and for the world's biggest magazines.

McGrath is able to show her work and shade range through the use of digital, expanding her message and setting an example for other artists to use a range of shades for any skin tone. McGrath never questioned that her brand would include inclusively and diversity and that it would be an integral pillar of the brand. McGrath pays careful attention to ensure the proper pigmentation and quality of every product. She proves this to be true by showing every product on every skin tone as much as possible.[78]

If you take a quick peak at her Instagram, McGrath Labs campaigns, and on the brand's website, there is no product that's shown on one skin tone. She represents all.

"It's about the colors working on every skin tone," she says in an interview with Fashionista, regarding how crucial it is for Labs to be diverse and inclusive when creating and launching. She also shares, "it's so important to know that you're not left out."[79]

This sets McGrath apart. She's able to access more people because she tailors her brand to be accessible to everyone.

---

78 "How Renowned Makeup Artist Pat McGrath Is Changing the Face of Beauty On Her Terms," Time.com, accessed August 1, 2020.

79 "Pat McGrath on Why Diversity and Inclusivity Have Been Crucial to Her Brand From Its Launch," Fashionista, accessed August 1, 2020.

Other beauty brands may still be lagging far behind the times. YSL missed the mark when they featured a dark-skinned woman wearing six shade switches of its "All Hour Concealer," all of which were clearly too light for her to wear. McGrath is authentic, employing diverse teams in the creation of her product as well as in marketing. She created a company evaluated recently at one billion dollars.[80]

McGrath shares in another interview with *Time* Magazine her thoughts on how the internet and social media have brought real growth in terms of beauty knowledge and beauty communities. "It's definitely changed the way we approach beauty," McGrath says, "It started out with magazines and all those incredible articles and no matter how steeped in beauty I would be, I would read a magazine and tear the page out and go straight to the store to buy exactly what I'd seen. With Instagram, it's taken it to a whole new level. You can see every minute, every second in your scroll, new ways of how to apply makeup, it's so entertaining and it's so inspiring." Not only does McGrath think you can find inspiration on how to apply makeup on social media, but she's been known to source models and even some of her staff through digital platforms.[81]

Her success comes from sticking to what she knows and doing it well. Some of the most important elements of McGrath and her work stem from her unique individuality and beauty, breaking away from traditional standards in the

80 Ibid.
81 "How Renowned Makeup Artist Pat McGrath Is Changing the Face of Beauty On Her Terms," Time.com, accessed August 1, 2020.

beauty world. McGrath values beauty beyond superficiality, looking at the story behind each person she sees.

Her upbringing gave her a different perspective to define beauty that comes from within, and it shows with the products she's created for all.

KEY TAKEAWAYS

SPARK:

Look within to who you are. McGrath realized her inspiration for building a beauty brand came from her mother and her childhood upbringing. This allowed McGrath to expand on those moments as a child watching Hollywood movie stars who became her main inspiration to create a career in makeup. Sometimes, your best idea is right in front of you.

SOCIAL:

McGrath used social media as a tool to be a resource. She's been interviewed many times on her thoughts around social media, explaining how digital changed the way we approach beauty as well as how she has approached it. We're able to reach more people, be entertained, and be inspired by how different people use makeup. Not only is McGrath using social media as a tool to sell her makeup, but she created a beauty line, employing diverse teams in the creation of her product to be inclusive to everyone. Not until 2020 have more brands taken a deeper look into their beauty lines, making sure their shades come in every color.

SECRET SAUCE:

There are a lot of people selling makeup on social media. I mean, I get served ads about new start-up companies all the time, dipping their toe into the pond. McGrath's secret sauce is the unique, innovative techniques she uses involving her hands when applying and experimenting with makeup. We all have something unique about ourselves, and when we find it, using our secret, unique powers can help lead us to big time success.

SUCCESS:

By the stories and events in McGrath's life, she was able to bring a different perspective on how to define beauty. So much so, she's estimated to be worth seven hundred million dollars. I would happily call that a major success!

CHAPTER 7

HOW SOCIAL MEDIA PRESENCE IS EVERYTHING | THE KATIE STURINO STORY

—

I had the emotional availability to put everything I had into a business, and what came out on the other side was better than I could have imagined.

-KATIE STURINO

If you have a strong voice and feel passionate about something, others will follow and want to be a part of that passionate community. It sounds really easy, but it's not.

Not everyone is going to find your voice unique or value what you bring to the table. The content you create on your page or specific campaigns centered around the powerful message you're trying to tell will help you gain traction, which in turn will help you grow your community faster. As we learned from McGrath, she was able to find her voice early on, growing a community in the fashion world with a different perspective. She used a different creative approach to makeup in ways no one did before and, because of that, she stood out from the crowd.

You grow your community through your unique perceptive. Your message has to be clear, because if it's not, how will you get others to follow you? You have to stand for something different. People want to be a part of something that they also feel strongly about, and now with social media, your unique perceptive can reach and resonate with more people than ever before.

I remember when, back in late 2017 (around when I got married), I found the cutest, most perfect romper that I really wanted to wear during my rehearsal dinner. The problem was, I knew the whole time wearing it my thighs would be sticking together because I'm not under one-hundred and twenty pounds nor am I one of those girls with a "thigh gap." Shout out to all my non-thigh gap women that are reading this book; the struggle is real.

I knew this outfit would leave me feeling uncomfortable in my own skin. I wished there was a product besides baby powder, which literally goes everywhere no matter what part of your body you're using it for, to fix my discomfort. Even my "normal" deodorant never worked for those areas, which makes sense because it wasn't designed to go between my thighs. Because of this, I knew the outfit would never work and proceeded out of the store, beyond frustrated and rethinking what type of outfit I was going to wear. It never crossed my mind that there should be a product specifically designed for women with this problem. So, I opted for a jumpsuit and called it a day.

Katie Sturino, founder of Megababe and fashion blogger behind *The 12ish Style* insisted she could build a business around creating a solution for thigh chafing. No one believed in her, even friends and family told her the idea was too niche of a product for a niche community. Whenever she went to factories to pitch her idea, she was often left explaining her idea to a lot of different men; can you even imagine? All I can think of is pitching this product to my dad and him just scratching his head and thinking I might have a concussion because the idea to him would be so out there. Sturino shares in an interview with *Elle* magazine, "They could not handle these topics. Some of them were like 'What's chafe? I don't think my wife has that.' Their general attitude was that it wasn't something they'd ever heard about; therefore it wasn't something that really has ever existed."[82] These words of discouragement did not stop Sturino from launching Megababe.

In June 2017, Sturino launched her now number-one seller, the Megababe Thigh Rescue anti-chafe stick, which sold out within a week of its launch. What a powerful move: having everyone tell you that your idea is stupid or that it's never going to catch the eyes of any consumer yet saying screw that

---

82 "Megababe Has Solutions for Beauty Problems We Don't Talk About. They Sell Out Immediately," ELLE, accessed August 22, 2020.

and going for it, anyway. As Sturino explains, "You have that little piece of doubt that's like: What if they're right? What if I'm making a product for myself, and now we've got thousands of units just sitting? What if chafing isn't a problem? When we did launch, it was a big exhale. We sold out and we made a product that people loved instantly."[83]

If you do a quick Google search, you'll find many competitors out there, but what makes Sturino's product different from the rest? For example, I'm sure you've heard of the company Anti Monkey Butts, right (laughing out loud)? I couldn't believe there was a company called this. First off, who would ever buy a product with a name like that? It sounds gross. And two, their messaging is all over the place. If you go to their website, they're trying to market their product for babies, women, men, athletes, farmers, and my personal favorite, professional drivers? Your messaging and who you are trying to target makes a difference. When I hear people say, "Well, my products are for everyone." Yes, your product could be used by a lot of different people, but who is your core buyer as well as your growth buyer? Different messages are going to reach different people, and that's extremely important when building a community and content to reach those people.

The most noticeable difference between the two brands is that Sturino is trying to stop people from feeling ashamed in their body, and her message is super clear; she has a consistent message and knows her target audience. You have less than five seconds to capture someone's attention when

---

83   Ibid.

scrolling through social media, and I can always tell without looking at the brand name if something's from Megababe's account. She's able to elevate her content to reach specific people with bright, modern packaging followers like and can relate to. Sturino's personal style also plays into the account, which fans love and goes back to eliminating personal shame. Sturino says in that same interview with *Elle* magazine,

"When you look at the colors, they're fun and happy. I'm a very colorful person. I wear prints. I feel like we picked the color palette because it's some of my favorite combinations of color."

Sturino created a product that had a solution for one of the hush-hush issues many women don't feel comfortable talking about. This is why she was able to grow such a strong community so quickly. She found her voice and was able to grow a community bringing attention to unaddressed issues that needed to be addressed.

But, Megababe didn't necessarily grow organically. You might be familiar with Sturino's personal style account on Instagram called The 12ish Style that helped jump-start Megababe to new heights of success. Her audience base is 95 percent female, and she's been able to bring those women on this business journey with her.

Sturino got her start working in public relations behind the scenes. She launched gigs at high-fashion companies like Dolce & Gabbana. While it sounds like the coolest dream gig ever, it wasn't an easy start. Sturino explains in an interview with *Fashionista* in 2019, "I really hated that environment; I found fashion people to be very humorless and very rude, and that was really hard for me," she admits. "I also think I felt out of place because of my size, a lot of the time; that's mental, and I was not in a place where I was comfortable. I was always the biggest person in the room; I couldn't fit into the samples at Dolce. I always felt uncomfortable, I think."[84]

This uncomfortable feeling didn't stop Sturino from starting her own PR firm at the young age of twenty-five. When I was that age, I was trying to figure out where the best brunch spots were in D.C. and if I could wake up early enough to grab a table without throwing up all the vodka shots I took the night before. Imagine having the entrepreneurial crops to think about starting a company at that age? She gained more influencer momentum when she started an Instagram page for her dog, Toast. Unfortunately, Toast passed away, but the account is still dedicated to former puppy mill dogs advocating for rescue.

This sparked Sturino's discovery that she could use social media to make changes of her own life. After getting leaving Dolce & Gabbana and then working for Bobbi Brown, Sturino decided she wanted to start setting up her own company. For ten years, she owned her own PR agency called Tinder. This became an issue when a new dating app decided to go by the same name.

When the new Tinder launched, she was getting so many inquiries from media and from people who couldn't find dates. Sturino ended up selling her website to Tinder because

84 "How Katie Sturino Went from Working in PR to Becoming an Influencer-Entrepreneur," Fashionista, accessed August 22, 2020.

of this and changed the title back to Katie Sturino PR. She used her dog, Toast, to get creative and started dressing her dog up in outfits like "who wore it better."[85]

Sturino saw opportunities; after all, she was a publicist. She thought, "We're near Oscar season, I'll try to dress Toast up in an Oscar look." Sturino had an outfit made by a woman on Craigslist and sent pictures around like a press release. It gained traction with people like Leandra Medine, who said to Sturino, "I love this, I'd love to do one with her," and that's what happened. She did a "who wore it better" with Medine. Others like Eva Chen saw it and thought it was hilarious. So much so that Chen wanted to do a funny comedy on it as the editor at *Lucky* Magazine. Because Sturino reframed her mindset to be the publicist of her own dog, this fun paid off. Toast became a fashion dog modeling for Karen Walker, getting married on "The Real Housewives," and she even wrote a book. This dog has a better life than me.

This experience showed Sturino a couple things, the main one was seeing the power of influence and the power of social media, and that using those powers could be a full-time career. This led to the launch of *The 12ish Style*. Because of her crafty PR skills, she was able to form a deeper relationship with Leandra Medine through *Man Repeller,* who wanted to do a style feature on Sturino. Sturino never thought this way about herself. As someone who was behind the scenes for so long, she couldn't imagine being in front of the camera.

---

85   Ibid.

Once Sturino started reading the comments from other women like "Oh my God, I've never seen my body type on a blog or on a social media site or like, in anything," Sturino wanted to change that. She had always felt this way. Sturino said, "Who's doing this? I'll do it. I'm always telling people where I'm buying stuff, and I'm always trying to give tips and hacks and fashion advice. I named it 'The 12ish' originally because I was a fluctuating person in a bigger space. So sometimes I was a twelve, sometimes a fourteen, and sometimes a sixteen; I think a lot of women in that size range slide up and down."

While it took some time getting used to being in front of the camera and really becoming confident showing this side of herself to the world (six months to be exact), people started to really connect with Sturino. "It took me awhile for it to come full circle for myself, because I was uncomfortable. But people right away—media people, women I talked to, friends—everyone got it right away."

It connected so quickly because Sturino's message was beyond just clothes and what she was wearing. She created a story of her own self-acceptance. Her message was so strong and powerful because it provided a place for women of all sizes to shop and find acceptance with their own bodies.

The success from her account continued when Sturino become outraged during a shopping trip when she wasn't able to buy anything in her size. Most fashion brands stop at size ten. Sturino realized that if you're outside of sizes 00-10 range, there is nothing to wear and options are very limited. In true Sturino fashion, she created a hashtag called #MakeMySize.

When coming across brands like Zimmermann, she took to social media to start a movement showing pictures of her in dressing rooms with outfits barely making it past her legs. This helped to bring awareness to these brands about how they should expand their sizing to include all different types of body shapes.

This message stuck, and reactions to it empowered so many women, landing her a community of 552,000 people. Sturino was able to bring light to a conversation that was well overdue. Because of her transparency and authenticity, her number one message was making women of all sizes feel comfortable in their own skin. She wanted to show there's more than one body type in this world, and it's okay that we're all different. She was able to attract and obtain a strong community quickly. This led to Megababe and the expansion of her product line. After her first product launch, Sturino has gone on to create award-winning products, including a rosy pits deodorant that, at one point, had a thirteen-thousand-person waitlist (wow).

Sturino was sick of using men's products (same here, girl), and because of the strong community she built, she was able to constantly have an open dialogue with her community. For example, she would ask her followers what they were using to make sweating "down there" more comfortable in the summertime. When Sturino noticed everything on the market was for men, for athletes, or was named something embarrassing and so cheesy (yes, we're looking at you Anti Monkey Butts), Megababe was born.

Social media platforms like Instagram have given people a place to connect and launch a product, just like Sturino did.

She was able to find her own unique voice by sharing her message around helping women feel good about themselves and growing an echo chamber for a safe space for women that didn't exist yet.

It's important to see how Sturino was able to grow and expand a community of women who for so long felt there was no one in their corner around this topic, including myself. I may not be in that size category, but it's important to note that the message was bigger than just one about products to help women feel like their best self. She disrupted the fashion industry by getting brands to think about expanding their sizing to include all women. She built everything around her main message and was able to grow her business, making lots of money. Nothing is more powerful than that.

Sturino's message was always clear, and she built products around those beliefs, growing her community and fan base. It's not enough to create a product anymore. Your message, voice, and the perspectives you have help bring a community of people together.

According to insider reports, Sturino is now worth upwards of five million. How's that for being too niche?

KEY TAKEAWAYS

SPARK:
Sturino became popular starting her Instagram page for her dog, Toast, and that sparked her idea to use it as a tool to build a business—a successful one highlighting what means the most: inclusivity for all body types.

SOCIAL:

Sturino was sick of not having clothes made in her size. Bringing awareness to the #MakeMySize campaign she started on social media helped her create products that truly helped women. She created a safe space for women that didn't exist discussing problems no one ever talked about before— organic growth on digital at its finest.

SECRET SAUCE:

Because Sturino's message was so powerful on social media, women quickly noticed the awareness she was bringing to all these brands, getting them to see how they should make different sizes for different types of body shapes. Expanding on that message, she was able to create a product that was able to help with chafing. So many people thought it wasn't a successful idea, yet she didn't listen and built a following on social media that led her to discover her unique perspective and bring it to a community of people, 549,000 people, to be exact.

SUCCESS:

Throughout this book, if I realized anything, it's that all these women have been super successful because the problem they're trying to fix is personal to them, and they created something that didn't exist yet. You have to start with the "why." Because Sturino was always clear and believed in the products she built, her community fan base keeps growing. Loving what you do is the real success. Being worth five million is just the icing on the cake.

CHAPTER 8

SECRET SAUCE – THE POWER OF INFLUENCE | THE DANIELLE BERNSTEIN STORY

"Be a fearless networker."

-DANIELLE BERNSTEIN

It's six o'clock on Thursday morning. Alarm clocks are going off, and women from all around the world are waking up, turning on their computers, and rushing to get their hands on influencer and entrepreneur Danielle Bernstein's newest collection with Macy's: The Danielle Bernstein Collection.

I had been waiting for this collection to launch for months, watching her Instagram stories on how the design process works, what goes into building a collection, and sneak peaks of what to expect. She had even asked her community for feedback on what to incorporate into the collection, and I felt fully invested in this collection, myself. I planned everything I wanted to buy the night before, making sure I got everything I wanted the next morning. I set my alarm but couldn't fall asleep; I was ready to make all my purchases. I was so prepared I literally had my credit card next to my bed. Committed or crazy, it didn't matter. I knew I had to have a piece from this collection.

The morning arrived, and I was devastated to learn one of my favorite pieces (a must-have on my list) was already sold out by seven o'clock in the morning. I couldn't believe it. I'm in EST, so how could that even be possible? I quickly remember her posting how the collection will be at select Macy stores around the US and frantically pulled up participating locations would be selling the collection. As my luck would have it, I had to be at work for an all-day client meeting. I thought to myself, "I hope and pray that by the time I leave work, some of the pieces I wasn't able to purchase online will still be available when I arrive after work." By the way, I've NEVER shopped at Macy's in my life.

For a moment, I paused and thought to myself, am I really taking time out of my day (and my bank account) to support someone I've never even met in life? This is a little crazy, right? I mean, this is someone who I've followed for years and felt like I grew up with. I was a part of this collection. I watched this collection start from the beginning to end. Danielle pulled her whole community into this experience, and everyone from her community felt like we were part of the amazing success about to take place. Throughout the day, when I had breaks between my meetings, I found myself rushing to my phone to see how the collection was doing, what was sold out, and how she exceeded sales only within a matter of hours. Her community (including me) was on this journey with her, and I wanted to support her no matter what.

And without questioning it anymore, I said, "absolutely I'm going to Macy's."

I've digitally grown up with Danielle. She created something so special with her community—something that takes time to build—and not everyone can achieve this type of success. So how did she grow this passionate community? What was her secret sauce to gaining this level of loyalty from her community? Two words: hustle and transparency.

The rise of influencers really didn't become a thing until 2006. This is when brands started to use influencers to help them reach their target audience and get in front of a community they might not have been able to reach, otherwise. Some people would even make the argument that influencers who were blogging early on and using the popular social platform, Instagram, had an easier time rising to the top. While that point might have some truth to it, it takes so much more than just posting a photo using hashtags to grow a community of over a million followers; you have to be different and stand out.

You have to find space in the market that doesn't exist yet. In an oversaturated industry, it's hard to stand out, so you have no choice but to be different. Take Danielle Bernstein; she has grown up with her followers and grown up, herself, on Instagram and in the public eye. From her style development to personal growth, she's shared everything with her community along the way.

Bernstein was born and raised in New York. Growing up, she was obsessed with clothes. She spent hours on her bedroom floor, cutting pages out of *Vogue* and taping collages to her walls. If you grew up in the late eighties or early nineties and didn't do this, did you even grow up in the nineties? Almost all my friends, including myself, had fashion, beauty, and celebrity pictures ripped out of magazines and hung all over our walls. However, unlike the rest of us that did grow up in the nineties, Bernstein took it a step further. She loved putting together looks with these ripped out pages from *Vogue*. All of her friends growing up seemed to know where she was headed except for herself.

She attended her first fashion show when she was just fifteen years old. This is where her love of fashion expanded into the passion she now has for what she does.

Bernstein was always set on moving to Manhattan to live the glamorous big city life that I feel like every girl wanted at some point (I mean who hasn't want to fulfill this dream? *Sex and the City* ... hello). But, Bernstein did it. When she was nineteen, she finally moved and found an apartment in Greenwich Village.

Before she permanently arrived in New York City, Danielle attended the University of Wisconsin. She realized quickly after arriving to the university it lacked classes in fashion. There was truly no fashion program, so Bernstein landed on the closest major to fashion—retail.

There were also no extracurricular activities for someone interested in fashion. The closest thing was a fashion club that only met twice a month, but Bernstein needed more. After flying home for winter break and hearing about her high school pal's adventures in the big city, Bernstein really started to feel that she was in the wrong place.

After a couple of months, Bernstein flew to Miami for the Ultra Music Festival with her boyfriend. She started unpacking clothes she hadn't worn all year due to the fact Bernstein felt she would have stood out like a sore thumb on campus. She felt good in these clothes. So, for the first time in a while, she felt like the person she wanted to be. As she began to talk with her boyfriend about an exit strategy in leaving Wisconsin, she knew what she had to do.

That night, Bernstein filled out an application to the Fashion Institute of Technology and within three weeks, a big envelope arrived with the word "ACCEPTED" inside. Bernstein finally got her wish to move to the big city and live out her dreams of making it in fashion.

In 2010 when Bernstein first arrived to FIT, she was blown away by the difference in how girls dressed for school. Bernstein describes FIT campus like a trip to the Metropolitan Museum of Art's costume exhibit. She talks in her book,

"This is Not A Fashion Story," about how her classmates made daring fashion choices. This is when the light bulb went off in Bernstein's head, or, as I like to call it, the spark that started it all:

"Wouldn't it be great for all my high school friends who were in all different states for college to have access to these styles? Or the girls around the world who weren't lucky enough to be around this trendy fashion every day?" [86]

With all of these thoughts floating in Bernstein's mind, she headed to a photographer store the next day and purchased her first point-and-shoot camera. Bernstein already had experience with blogging when she created *Speak of Chic* back in Wisconsin, a text-only blog as a way to keep close to fashion. She needed to create another platform like *Speak of Chic*. This time, Bernstein's blog needed to expand from just text to both text and images, showing people the styles on FIT's campus she got to experience every day. Before launching her website, she needed to create a URL before doing anything else. Without thinking about it for too long, her fingers typed in the words "WeWoreWhat," and, to Bernstein's surprise and excitement, it was available.

WeWoreWhat began as a street-style blog on which she posted the photos she took of outfits around FIT's campus, so she could give that outfit inspiration to her friends back at her previous college. But people started emailing her asking where they, too, could get these same outfits, and Bernstein

86 Danielle Bernstein and Emily Sigel, This Is Not a Fashion Story: Taking Chances, Breaking Rules, and Being a Boss in the Big City (North Charleston, Vertel Publishing, 2020).

had to spend hours finding out if items weren't available anymore, or better yet, too expensive for the "average" person.

Bernstein couldn't believe how many readers she already had just from word of mouth. She always thought of her blog as something fun that she was passionate about. Never in a million years did she think this would turn into a million-dollar brand. In 2011, everything changed when Bernstein expanded to taking street-style photos beyond FIT's campus and into places like New York City's fashion week. Bernstein recalled scrolling through her DSLR to review all the amazing shots she got on her camera when, all of a sudden, she was asked by a photographer to take her photo. This changed everything for Bernstein.

Eventually, as her personal style was resonating with more readers, she flipped the camera around to herself and made WeWoreWhat a personal style blog. After noticing she was blogging more than paying attention in class, she decided to take two semesters off to focus full-time on her blog. But before doing so, she had to give the biggest pitch of her life— to her dad.

After her dad's blessing, Bernstein hit the ground running trying to prove to her dad this risk was going to be worth it.

A year into her blog, Danielle started to realize this could become a business. Slowly but surely, brands started reaching out to send her their products to post and promote on her page. She reached out to a talent agency who helped her transform her blog into a legitimate business. For those of you who don't know what a talent agency is, think of it as a specific person at a company who is going to pitch you to brands to make you more money. These agencies have connections to get influencers more exposure and more money, but that comes with a heavy price, of course. For example, Bernstein's agent takes twenty percent of all profit from deals.[87]

At one point during her early blogging days (2012), Bernstein downloaded Instagram. According to Bernstein, it took months for her to realize there could be a tie between her blog and this new social media platform. One night, Bernstein posted a picture of her and a friend wearing the same outfit, and the post got four hundred likes and sixteen comments in less than thirty minutes. It doesn't sound like a lot now, but back in 2012, this was a big deal. No longer were her fans having to type into their browser to find Bernstein's popular blog. We could all have instant access to her street styles from our pockets. Bernstein started tagging the brands she was wearing as well creating hashtags to generate more followers and views. These strategic decisions eventually paid off.

From now on, she would shift most of her time to building a community of people through Instagram.

---

87 Ibid.

Word of month spreads fast—especially on social media. You can easily be rewarded for being completely transparent in gaining a bigger following and reaching more people. Bernstein prides herself on this. No influencer had ever said how much money they were paid for partnerships and working with brands. Once Bernstein did an interview revealing that she could made upwards of five to twenty-five thousand dollars per Instagram post, she quickly noticed how much she jumped up in followers.[88]

While turning her Instagram account into a business, Danielle knew she needed to brand herself beyond the influencer title. She wanted to be more than an influencer promoting other brands on her platform. She wanted to find a niche that didn't exist yet. She needed to find that secret sauce that would help her grow her platforms even more.

After Danielle worked with both luxury and high street retailers, she saw an opportunity to fill a gap in the market for a niche but old-school staple. Danielle saw this staple always popping up in brand collections but always off—too over the top, not the right fit, etc. She wanted to create a modern overall that fit well but maintained the original DNA of vintage styles. Danielle had always been inspired by the versatility and the ease of overalls. What was once a traditional utilitarian work uniform is now a style that can be worn to a cocktail party or while causally running errands.

---

88 "Danielle Bernstein Gets Real About Money And The Power of Influence," Daily Front Row, accessed August 22, 2020.

In 2016, her dream came true. Danielle launched her first collection, Second Skin Overalls; the tagline of *WeWoreWhat* was originally "overalls are my second skin." It took her four months and one hundred thousand dollars of her own savings to become ready to launch. The help of Bernstein's following on Instagram landed her selling seven hundred thousand dollar's worth of product within the first hour of her launching on her Instagram account. By the end of the day, Bernstein's collection was sold out.[89]

One of Bernstein's biggest success factors in launching her overalls was keeping her customer service in her control, especially on social media. It's so important to know what your community loves about your product, what they wish it had, and how it can be better. Knowing this helped Bernstein tweak and produce better designs which is why, after releasing five collections and grossing over thousands of dollars, the brand was super successful before it was re-branded as SSO by Danielle.

In an interview, Bernstein says she gets asked all the time, "What's the secret?" and she states "I always say that my product is an example of organic growth. I was an authentic young woman, living in New York City, trying to make it like everyone else, and I was showing that in a really raw and real way. So, I think people could relate to me. My blog is a mix of the relatable and the aspirational. I don't only write about my style. I talk about where I'm eating, going out, vacationing, I

---

89 "How 'We Wore What' Blogger Danielle Bernstein Went From Sophomore To Seven Figures In Under 6 Years," Forbes, accessed August 22, 2020.

offer business advice… Sharing in that authentic way is how I gained such a good relationship with my audience."[90]

Bernstein disrupts the fashion industry not only because of what she wears, the styles she creates, and trends she sets, but because of the strong community standing behind her. In the last ten years, Danielle built a passionate community on digital platforms reaching over two million people. Early on, Danielle branded herself as a native New Yorker, a young entrepreneur, and a twenty-something-year-old just trying to make it like everyone else.

With a saturated market in the fashion space, it's so important to find your niche, and that's exactly what Danielle Bernstein did.

KEY TAKEAWAYS
SPARK:
I honestly can say I never really thought about any go-to brand for overalls. Bernstein created one. She saw an opportunity to fit into a space that didn't exist yet. She used her personal love for overalls to make them into a staple needed in any and every wardrobe.

SOCIAL:
You can say Bernstein was early to the Instagram party and becoming one of the early influencers is why she was so

---

90   "Danielle Bernstein Gets Real About Money And The Power of Influence," Daily Front Row, accessed August 22, 2020.

successful, but she (early on, when no one talked about how much money they would make) revealed how much money she could make on just one Instagram post. People found this appealing, and her community grew overnight to the millions. Nowadays on social media, being transparent sells more than any dollar amount you throw behind a post.

SECRET SAUCE:

Bernstein prides herself on being authentic and uses her story to grow her products in an organic way. She wants her brand to be relatable and aspirational in all the clothes she designs and the projects she's involved in.

SUCCESS:

As we've talked about in this book, there are many beauty and fashion brands. There are also many influencers trying to leave the real world's career paths, instead following the digital career path and making it as influencers. People think it's easy, but it's not. Bernstein's success comes from constantly staying connected to her community and designing products for which she knows her community is waiting. She talks a lot about community and how important it is. If she didn't, she wouldn't be where she is today.

CHAPTER 9

SUCCESS – GROW YOUR BRAND AND START WINNING | THE EMILY WEISS STORY

—

"It takes a lot more than a great product to make a great brand."

EMILY WEISS

We all have our own beauty routines, and mine consist mostly of Glossier's products. Glossier's lightweight foundations, amazing face masks, and, we can't forget, the incredible boy brow are all now a staple in my daily routine thanks to Emily Weiss, founder of Glossier.

With over 2.7 million Instagram followers, Glossier has been named a top beauty brand by many beauty experts like *Allure, Teen Vogue, Glamour, Nylon, Women's Wear Daily,* and *Cosmopolitan.*

With a list of awards like the 2015 Digital Innovator of the Year award and recognition by Fast Company as one of its Most Innovative Companies of 2017, Weiss and Glossier are changing the way we see beauty. Weiss is often credited for turning traditional beauty retail on its head by cracking the code for selling makeup directly to consumers through Instagram.[91] No more days of begging your mom to take you to a beauty counter to get information on the newest trends and must-haves; it's all available in your pocket.

Weiss was able to get an idea from starting a conversation around beauty products with women and understanding what they were looking for in beauty products.

By fostering these open conversations, Weiss created products based on consumer feedback. She's able to create a blog of content from real women and influencers and distribute it to millions of readers all centered around one topic: beauty. She created a community of women passionate about beauty, tips and tricks, what works, what doesn't, and questions that were finally being answered. These topics were never

---

91 "The Glossier Marketing Machine: How Emily Weiss Hacked Culture to Build a $100 Million Business That's Disrupting Beauty," Jumper Media, accessed March 28, 2020.

talked about or discussed in this matter; this was a niche that needed to be filled, and Weiss had a plan. Weiss was aware that all of those thousands of readers were potential customers, so what better way than to create products they want? Weiss wasn't the only influencer and brand following this strategy. Many others in the beauty and fashion industry were following suit.

In 2018, Glossier sold one of their famous boy brows every thirty-two seconds.[92] We have now entered a new wave of influencer marketing. Influencer marketing is no longer something brands smirk at or don't notice. It's now more mature, savvier, and grown-up, and equipped with the know-how and skills to help brands connect in meaningful ways with demographics they want. In fact, nearly sixty percent of marketers say they are going to increase their influencer marketing budgets in 2020.[93] Not only are more brands investing in influencer marketing, but influencers themselves are creating brands through their own personal brands and companies on social media platforms like Instagram, TikTok, and YouTube. Influencers, with their strong networks and the army-built community around them, are able to socially listen to that community and create products they know the consumer wants.

Who is Emily Weiss? She's a woman who built an empire connecting beauty product lovers to beauty essentials, easy-to-use skincare, and makeup that is now the backbone of many women's routine.

---

92 "Glossier Is Launching a New Brow Product to Accompany Boy Brow," Harper's BAZAAR, accessed March 28, 2020.

93 "60% of Marketers Say Influencer Budgets Will Stay the Same or Increase Post-COVID-19," Talking Influence," accessed March 28, 2020.

Originally, the world met Weiss back in 2007. She first landed on our television screens during the second season of *The Hills*. Twelve years later, she built an empire that broke every boundary in the beauty industry and is valued at 1.2 billion dollars—not bad for a five-year-old start-up all starting from a blog titled *Into the Gloss*.[94]

Weiss started her career walking the halls at Chanel as a part-time employee, while balancing a full course load at New York University. Her boss, Eva Chen, at the time an editor in Chanel's beauty department and now Instagram's director of fashion partnerships, said that Weiss "had that X factor. She was a college student who clearly had a plan, so pulled together and focused, which was so different from me at that age." As Weiss got older, working in the world and meeting many different women, she became interested in how beauty can bring very different people together. She explains "It's interesting, because with fashion, there's not so many people in the world who might have the same t-shirt, or something that happens to be in the market for a spring/summer season, whereas with a beauty product—take Maybelline Great Lash for example; there's barely a woman I know who hasn't at some point tried Maybelline Great Lash, from all different countries, ages, or socioeconomic backgrounds. Beauty is an interesting connective tissue that allows women to share and to come together."[95]

---

94 "The Glossier Marketing Machine: How Emily Weiss Hacked Culture to Build a $100 Million Business That's Disrupting Beauty," Jumper Media, accessed March 28, 2020.

95 "A Decade in Digital: Emily Weiss Wants Into the Gloss and Glossier to Be About More than Product," Fashionista, accessed March 28, 2020.

In 2010, Weiss talked about a conversation she had when on a shoot in Miami with model Doutzen Krosesa in a trailer, a common conversation spot during a shoot. At some point in their conversation, Krosesa described an amazing self-tanner she loved, and Emily realized she had never used a self-tanner in her life. Krosesa explains "you exfoliate this way, put it on, and it's like air foam, doesn't smell and not like the rest because it's super easy to use and goes onto the skin perfectly."[96]

As Weiss listened to her explain this amazing self-tanner, all she thought about was running to the store after this shoot and grabbing some, which is exactly what she did. She ran into a CVS near where she was staying for the summer and rushed home to try it out, herself. After an amazing experience with her new self-tanner, she wanted to write about her experience. She felt others needed to know. She also felt a need to continue passing along a positive review since she'd heard about it from a personal recommendation, too. It was her civic duty to share this with the world.

The next day, Weiss went to the beauty editor at *Vogue*, Sarah Brown. And real quick side note, Brown is a legend at *Vogue*, so I can't even begin to describe how much courage that took to do at the age of twenty-two. To ask someone at that level to give you a chance on a piece you want to write in a completely different department at a well-established magazine is what I like to call "badass." You go, girl! Weiss hadn't met Brown yet, but she was eager and persistent to get this beauty secret out. She asked Brown if she could write a small piece on the *Vogue* website about a self-tanner she just discovered and explained

---

96   Ibid.

the need she felt to write this story. If Brown gave Weiss the opportunity to write this story and she liked it, *Vogue* would publish it so readers around the world could have access to this information; information that started between only two people now could be shared with millions. Brown gave Weiss the green light to write the post, and later, it was published online.

It was such a cathartic moment in Weiss's life. This moment was important because it was the first time she felt passionate enough about a product to want to have a conversation around it. This wasn't something she felt ever before talking about a shirt or another piece of clothing. This is when she caught the bug. As Weiss continued to work as a fashion assistant at *Vogue*, she was dreaming up an even bigger piece to write, something that would connect millions of people around the world: a beauty blog called *Into the Gloss*.

Weiss stated,

> "*I wanted to start this new conversation around product that was more through the lens of personal style, rather than beauty coming from a product—or launch-driven perspective; really talking about the best of beauty as it relates to women's routines, women's opinions, as women's individual, unique beauty thumbprints.*"[97]

What's interesting is that Weiss didn't create a new beauty product that wasn't on the shelves (yet), but rather she recreated how we think and talk about beauty. There's no single

---

97   "A Decade in Digital: Emily Weiss Wants Into the Gloss and Glossier to Be About More than Product," Fashionista, accessed March 28, 2020.

thing that's best in beauty. My favorite lipstick could be the best for me, but someone else could feel a completely different lipstick works better for them. She was fascinated by this discovery. Instead of creating a "what's new" in beauty, she created a platform where millions of people can relate to beauty and turned it into a community. She created something more than just a blog. Itt was more like a social platform, fostering two-way conversations with content and comments read by hundreds to thousands of people each week.

Nowadays, you can livestream on most any platform, giving you instant content at your fingertips, but imagine back in 2010 when livestreaming wasn't an option yet. Can you believe there was a time when magazine and print was where most people sourced their beauty inspiration? There's no other feeling to have but liberation from a content perspective—being able to reach millions of women within a matter of hours—the biggest benefit of having a digital presence. Weiss wanted to spark a real conservation with real women about what products they love, how to achieve the perfect skin tone, and other topics on which so many people had been craving dialogue.

This got me thinking about beauty products as an industry, and the industry creates a true need for interaction and dialogue. Who doesn't love to experiment with beauty products and share this experience with their closest girlfriends?

If you're reading this, I bet instead of going to a brand's website or a celebrity profile, you've asked your closest friends what they use and for their favorite beauty products. We look to our own communities for advice, and this is what Weiss centered her blog around. I, for one, love to change up my beauty products, and I'm always looking for something inexpensive, able to provide full-day coverage, free of animal cruelty, etc., always looking for that next best thing to make me feel beautiful and confident. I love being able to go online and get advice on what products that might work best for me and reading how different products effected different people. We've become picky as consumers about what we'll put on our bodies and faces, and what better way than to bring a community together than by connecting those who all share these same beliefs?

Bringing together a community is just one piece of the puzzle. Tied to bringing a community together is creating content that keeps your community interested and talking. When starting the blog, Weiss needed to come up with content ideas to share with her readers within the different areas of content she was interested in creating. A popular content series she started was "Top Shelf," where subjects were interviewed in their bathrooms and captured photos of their bathroom shelves and medicine cabinets.

Notable interviews included Jenna Lyons (now 37.9 thousand Instagram followers) and Karlie Kloss (now 8.6 million Instagram followers), both connections she made while working in the fashion industry. While working with these models, she asked about their beauty routines and if she could interview them and share what they were using. Doing this allowed her to gather exclusive content for millions to access around the world. The interviews were successful, reaching over one-and-a-half million unique visitors since their posting. In response to the popularity of her social media content, the hashtag #ITGTopShelfie was created, allowing ordinary women to be discovered and interviewed for the column.[98] Every woman could feel included no matter your shape, skin, or size.

While building *Into the Gloss*, Weiss knew she could create products that didn't exist in the market using community feedback. She could build better products inspired by her direct relationship to consumers online. Most brands introduce people to their brand to then build a customer base, but since Weiss already had a customer base through *Into the Gloss*, it was now time to introduce her brand, Glossier, to her customer base.

Weiss was successful because she did two things really well: branding and social media. Combining the two was a recipe for success. If you're a big Glossier fan, then you know that the color pink is EVERYWHERE. It's become so iconic Glossier created the hashtag #glossierpink, tagged on twenty-four thousand posts on Instagram.[99] Hashtags are important in Glossier's strategy, making it easy for fans to find content and share it with their inner circle. This also keeps everything in one place, making it easy for the internal team to engage with fans. There's something so special about a brand responding

---

98 "#ITGTopShelfie Archives - Into The Gloss." Into The Gloss, accessed March 28, 2020.

99 "#glossierpink Hashtag on Instagram," Instagram.com, accessed March 28, 2020.

to you in that it can make you feel seen and heard—especially when it's a brand you're passionate about.

Weiss listened to what her customers wanted through social listening, a fancy way of saying she found conversations happening on social about her products. She created innovative ways to reach her top fans. She even created a Slack channel with one hundred of Glossier's top customers for weekly updates on products. This allowed Glossier's team to create products based on real feedback ending with the ultimate payoff: keeping their audience coming back to buy more products.

Weiss talks about how she created a product completely based off this Slack channel, **the Milky Jelly Cleanser**. Because they loved this product so much, members of the channel wanted to show it off on social media.

This was a great way for Glossier to collect free content to repost on their channels, helping them create editorial plans, prioritize their content, and get ahead. You'll also notice *Into the Gloss*'s and Glossier's content are both super authentic to who they are as brands, shooting their photos on iPhones rather than on a DSLR camera. Because of this approach, the brand feels more natural and more relatable, and we as consumers feel a stronger connection to be open and share within this community. *Forbes* found sixty-two percent of millennials stated if a brand engages with them on a personal level through social media, they're more likely to show loyalty to that brand.[100]

---

100 "10 New Findings About The Millennial Consumer," Forbes, accessed March 28, 2020.

Weiss excels at listening to her customers and talking to her community like we're all BFFs. Don't underestimate the power of authenticity, being open to feedback, and changing to make a better product for your customer. Because, ultimately, the customers are going to keep you in business and help you to continue to grow your brand.

Weiss spent four years building a community before she ever built a brand. Extending her reach further, she created a pop-up Glossier location, eventually turning into a permanent location in the spring of 2018. A location with dreamy dessert vibes in the middle of a popular and famous street in Los Angeles? It is easy for me to already picture all the basic betches running to check it out. I mean, who doesn't want to shop and take cool pictures pretending like you're in the Antelope Canyon in Arizona? Sign me up.

The success here is found in creating a unique space for the community you built to take part in a shared experience. This also allowed her audience to take content and distribute it to their own communities, educating more people about Glossier products and leaving Emily with zero dollars spent on marketing. You don't get the same excitement from people when they know they're being sold to, but when you start with building a community to solve a problem together with products based around customer feedback, your growth will flourish organically.

#GLOSSIERCANYON

It's a sunny day in Los Angeles, and I'm sitting on the floor with some of my closest friends from high school for a girls trip, putting my best face forward to have a fun-filled day exploring the city. As we're about to walk out the door, my girlfriend turns to me and says "your eyebrows look so good. What do you use?" Sure enough, before leaving, we paused for a moment so I could quickly do hers. Within minutes of the application going onto her brows, she fee.s immediate satisfaction in how natural her eyebrows look and in how a product finally achieved the results she was looking for without breaking the bank. This product gives you a hint of volume, making the features on your face stand out. Luckily, there is a pop-up shop on Melrose Pl., so we rush to visit and explore all the products Glossier had to offer.

When we get there, I am shocked to see we have to wait in a ten-minute line just to get into the store.

Once we're in, the store is packed—women and men all over the store, pushing each other and crowding around every single product. Not only is this just store, but this pop-up is doused in millennial pink, pampas grass in every corner, and broken concrete or clay with modern fixtures to pull off an eclectic look. The store looks more like an art exhibit than a beauty store. This place is screaming for you to show off that you've been to Glossier's newest pop-up store on Instagram (I'm thinking to myself this is genius marketing), creating a space that lets your consumers create buzz for you they also feel connected to. Even once we get into the store, we wait in another line just to see the fake canyon. Yes, you read that correct: a fake canyon.

Glossier wanted to keep to its brand's mission to create an experience rather than just another retail store. This experience was known as the "selfie canyon," quickly earning its very own hashtag, #glossiercanyon. And if you're wondering if I waited in another line to see a fake canyon, the answer is abso-freakin-lutely.

The space was so dreamy, and I couldn't wait to share it with my friends. It wasn't just about the beauty products; it was more than that. I wanted to capture the experience I had with my friends and post something Insta-worthy to share, something I know my community would be interested in (I know, great marketing, right?). The store left me feeling inspired (because, let's be real, I was picking out ideas for my own house designs), but I truly felt like I found a brand whose mission was to put their customers first.

Before Glossier ever had a pop-up store, the blog *Into the Gloss* allowed a for a similar community to come together to share their experience with beauty products while having the power of each individual to choose their own style. We're done, as a society, allowing brands to tell us what we need. We want trusting connections to relatable people with real experiences using these products to inspire us to be who we want to be, and Weiss did that while disrupting a whole industry.

Beauty is a huge industry—a four-hundred-and-fifty-billion-dollar global market—and it's going to be worth seven-hundred-and-fifty billion in six years.[101] Why is that? It's because of social media, because of sharing, and because of the ability

101 "Global Beauty and Personal Care Product Market Is Expected to Reach USD 756.63 Billion by 2026 : Fior Markets," GlobeNewswire News Room, accessed March 28, 2020.

to have digital conversations. Beauty is not held tightly by the women behind the Lancôme beauty counter anymore. Women going into Sephora or Ulta are pulling out their iPhones and texting their friends "What was that product you were telling me that makes my lips look 5 times bigger?"

THIS IS HOW THINGS WORK, NOW. THIS IS THE NEXT WAVE.

Weiss built a platform giving people a voice through beauty. You might find it hard to shop online for makeup and beauty products, but when searching on YouTube for "glossier boy brow," you'll come across multiple videos of different women of varying shapes and skin tones sharing their experiences with the product. You can visualize how the product will look on you.

Social media allowed us to connect to one another in a way we haven't been able to be connected before, especially in the beauty industry. Weiss built a digital community, shaping the way she created a successful company through the consumer's end.

KEY TAKEAWAYS

SPARK:

You never know what conversations can turn into a business. Focus on things you are passionate about. Be open to new opportunities coming into the picture and take a look at pain points or struggles you feel passion about fixing. Listen to the people around you and what their pain points are. Weiss wanted to build a community of connections between a previously disconnected audience. Just like she needed to tell the story of her amazing experience with self-tanner to the world, she thrived on creating something for the end user and it being a successful experience for the consumer. Find where you catch "the bug."

SOCIAL:

Social media is a powerful tool and can be used to influence people's purchasing decisions by the content you create and distribute. Weiss said Instagram helped the brand tremendously. Glossier-produced content combines how-to, funny, relatable memes specific to beauty issues and the products, themselves. With ample amount of user-generated content to authenticate the company's products and posts, this content creates conversations. Your content should create something for your audience. If it doesn't, you shouldn't post it.

SECRET SAUCE:

Consistency is key when it comes to branding and social media. Leverage activations you can create on social media like branded specific hashtags (making it easier for all your content to be in one place), user-generated content campaigns, or giveaways. An important note is that customer feedback played a large role in shaping this brand and how they innovated their products with a customer-first approach. Being super authentic to those values helped create a successful brand.

SUCCESS:

Weiss took a different approach to success. She led with a community-first approach, putting the product second. The areas in which she thrived were building a foundation around customers first, engaging content, two-way conversations, and community. Each category played a role in the success of *Into the Gloss's* and Glossier's brandings and positions on social media. Being authentic to who you are as a brand and to your customers is rewarding. There's an even bigger reward in achieving Weiss's level of this success; she made four hundred million dollars in four years in business.[102]

---

102 "How Glossier Turned Into a $400 Million Business in Four Years," Product Habits, accessed March 28, 2020.

PART 3

THE DIGITAL DILEMMA

CHAPTER 10

THE FUTURE OF DIGITAL

Being connected digitally is more important than ever before. Going through a pandemic (COVID-19) has definitely shown all of us that if you're not on digital or providing some sort of connection through digital, you likely won't make it.

eMarketer has upped their 2020 projections for time spent on social due to the coronavirus. Previously, they were expecting social time spent to remain consistent for the next few years, but now they've dramatically increased expected usage time. For context, in November they initially projected a six-second increase from 2019 to 2020, and now that has increased to nearly seven minutes.

With more and more people spending less time commuting to work, there's going to be an interruption to digital audio's growth. Of those aged eighteen and older who use social networks at least once per month, time spent with each medium includes all time spent with that medium source, according to eMarketing findings.[103]

---

103 "US Time Spent with Media 2020," EMarketer, accessed August 22, 2020.

NANO INFLUENCERS, AKA NEWBIE INFLUENCERS, ON THE BLOCK

We've talked a lot of bigger names in this book, but it's not all about the big names in the fashion and beauty industries. The rise of nano-influencers came too, as they've been able to take advantage of higher engagement among their audience.

Engagement is up with nano-influencers because they charge significantly less than celebrities or popular influencers with large followings.

Nano-influencers have between one and ten thousand followers and can sometimes be a challenge to work with given the number of fake accounts on social media.

Along with nano-influencers, advanced tracking tools, like Facebook Pixel, make it possible to chart out the buyer's journey, leading to more sales. However, to make this strategy effective, you need to keep publishing good content regularly.

Facebook is the leading platform for product discovery. Instagram and Pinterest are closely catching up in this trend. Anyone looking to grow into the beauty and fashion industries through social media should be looking at these three platforms.[104]

I remember a time when Facebook's algorithm would emphasize meaningful interactions. Asking people to 'love' if you would wear this on date night on social posts would help

---

104 Shane Barker, "The Future of Social Media Marketing – 11 Trends That Will Impact Your Business (Updated May 2020)," accessed August 22, 2020).

generate conversations. Now, in 2020, that's not enough. Moving away from engagement baiting techniques and into genuine content for your brand is the key to success in the future of social media marketing. [105]

OUR FUTURE CONTENT ON DIGITAL: AUGMENTED REALITY

During the pandemic, using AR filters have been even more popular with people stuck at home with nothing to do. These filters on Instagram, Facebook, or Snapchat, who have all copied each other at this point, give you options to change your face to different looks. According to a Coresight Research report, consumer spending on reality technologies was projected to reach seven billion dollars in 2020, even before COVID-19, but they predict the pandemic could drive even higher adoption of AR (and VR) tech.[106]

As a social media manager, I've already had to get creative with digital tools around my company's brand to reach consumers. Similarly, at the same time, more people are spending more time on their phones and on social platforms. Augmented reality is emerging as a bigger part of the future for many of these social media channels. Beauty and fashion brands should take advantage of these merging features to stay relevant and help them produce content at a lower cost.

Back in 2018, AR try-on was already changing the future of shopping. Brands like Dior and Warby Parker made at-home

---

105 Ibid.

106 "Pandemic Could Lead to Higher AR, VR Adoption," Retail Dive, accessed August 22, 2020.

AR "try-ons" a norm. With shoppers at home, AR clothing is getting an even bigger boost. According to *Vogue Business*, many brands are turning to augmented reality to take online shopping to the next level.[107]

SOCIAL MEDIA IS TAKING ALL MY MONEY

With the recent introduction to Instagram shopping, consumers can now buy directly through the platform, creating another arm for e-commerce and retail brands. They can start selling on Instagram without having to funnel followers to a biography link.

We don't see this growth with just Instagram, since LinkedIn's ad platform recently evolved to help B2B brands get their products in front of relevant customers.

VIDEO CONTENT - ALL DAY ERR DAY

Long-form and short-form video content are among the most shared content on social media. YouTube is second only to Facebook in terms of active users. Although Instagram might be regarded as the top hub for influencers, more and more brands and marketers are flocking to YouTube in masses.[108]

Instagram stories are now a staple in your social media strategy. Hashtags can generate more engagement and discovery on your page.

---

107 "Why Brands Need to Have an Augmented Reality Plan to Reach Young Consumers – YPulse," 2020. Ypulse.com, accessed August 22, 2020.

108 "The Most Important Social Media Trends to Know for 2020," Sprout Social, accessed August 22, 2020.

SOCIAL MEDIA IS HERE TO STAY

Social media will always be forever changing. There will always be new social channels, platforms, new strategies to test, and new tools within platforms to help you gain more and more popularity. It's worked for all these women in this book to use it as a strategy and tool to achieve success.

While social media is important to any marketing strategy, there's a lot you can do with social media, either to help or to hurt you. It's important to know these trends to keep up with the future of digital. You want to continue innovating yourself and your brand. If we've learned anything, it's that keeping a community engaged and growing is hard work.

Stay true to who you are because these trends will only leverage you to be who you truly were all along and, and, in turn, your brand will succeed.

CHAPTER 11

CANCELING "CANCEL CULTURE"

Staying relevant is not an easy task. Finding ways to innovate your brand, not just with products but everything in your life, is tough.

The women I've talked about in this book figured out how to keep readers engaged—in their content, products, beliefs, and their personal journeys. New seasons create new trends and new beauty products, meaning you're always expanding your brand, and it's a LOT.

So what happens when it becomes too much? What happens if you make a mistake?

You're in the public eye to millions of people around the world. People can hide behind a computer screen to judge your every move, and trust me, they'll definitely let you know their feelings and thoughts via the comment section or direct message. That's a lot of pressure, so having thick skin in this game is a must.

You've probably seen the hashtag #cancelculture start popping up on social media. What does this mean? Cancel culture refers to the popular practice of withdrawing support for (essentially canceling) public figures, influencers, and brands after they have done or said something considered objectionable or offensive.[109]

Being canceled is equivalent to walking into a war zone and then realizing you're alone with no one else behind you. No matter what mistakes you want to handle privately, there's nowhere to run. "Everyone seems to assume that influencers and celebrities alike are powerful, with superhuman resilience and unsurmountable abilities to rise above trolling. Ultimately though, we're all humans and when it comes down to it, influencers are just as powerless towards trolls as the rest of us. In the face of bullying and slander, we all become victims—no matter how many Louis Vuitton bags you own, or how many holidays you go on every year," said Sedge Beswick, global senior social media manager at online fashion retailer, ASOS.[110]

Beswick's main goal is to ensure ASOS is leading and innovating within the digital space, guaranteeing ASOS is where the consumers are. She talks about how being "cancelled" is an incredibly isolating experience, and it's important that brands stand by their morals in our increasingly political

---

109 "Cancel Culture." Dictionary.com, accessed August 22, 2020.
110 "How Can Brands Working with Influencers Safeguard against 'Cancel Culture,'" The Drum, accessed August 22, 2020.

world. "Be the bigger person, the bigger voice and better humans," she tells *The Drum*.[111]

We're quick to judge as a society. Cancel culture on social media has become particularly rampant in the beauty industry. Kim Kardashian was almost canceled after initially naming her shapewear line "Kimono," which social media users deemed culturally insensitive. At this point, the Kardashian/Jenner clan has more money than Bill Gates, and having lots and lots of money can help you remove a mistake. For indie brands, it's a harder recovery; they can't just buy their audience back or divert the conversation with a shiny new product.

Far too often we're here for the drama and not diverting the conversation to education. Avoiding negativity online is the most challenging thing because, let's be honest, who doesn't like following a heated debate on social media? I find myself all the time following @dietprada or @bethereinfive with Kate Kennedy, a Chicago-based entrepreneur and a pop culture commentator who I love listening to because she's entertaining. It's juicy, and it's fun to be in the know with what's going on in pop culture. But empowering people feels so much better than spreading hate.

Danielle Gronich, co-founder of CLEARstem Skincare, says "Psychology tells us that we are very poor judges of other peoples' motives. A perceived motive is usually our own projection. So, if you have to assume, assume the best. If someone really offends you, unfollow them. The best revenge is no

---

111 Ibid.

revenge. When you wrestle with pigs, you both get dirty, but the pig likes it. Spend that energy better, by educating and spreading awareness."[112]

I'm not saying that there aren't benefits to holding influencers and brands accountable and monetarily supporting the people with whom you align. What it comes down to is people just wanting to support brands they believe in. Where it gets dangerous is not allowing any room for growth, whether it be on the brand side or on the founder side. Social media spreads fast, and once it's out there, people can sometimes jump to conclusions without knowing all the facts up front.

Danielle Bernstein, the founder and CEO of *WeWoreWhat* who I talked about earlier in this book, has recently come under a lot of fire on social media. Bernstein, first, was ripped to pieces on Instagram over stealing a design idea from a small business owner. The design? A mask with a chain on it. I had already seen many masks with chains on them flowing around social media, so when the news broke, I was definitely skeptical. As I scrolled through the photos showing the receipts on what happened, it didn't look so good for Bernstein.

The first to break the story was @DietPrada, who is notorious for shaming brands, designers, and others for fashion copycatting, often from stories and DMs from Instagram followers tipping them off with new content. You can think of them as the industry watchdog, AKA the fashion police.[113]

---

112 "What Indie Beauty Brand Founders Make Of Cancel Culture - Beauty Independent," Beauty Independent, accessed August 22, 2020.

113 "We're All Drinking Diet Prada Now," The New York Times, accessed August 22, 2020).

DietPrada shared multiple posts including screenshots of Bernstein having an exchange in conversation with brand By Second Wind, the designer DietPrada claimed Bernstein ripped off. The posts showed Bernstein reaching out to the brand via DM on June 29, 2020. On July 2, she messaged again with a heads up... she was also launching her own masks.

When I reviewed the posts, I noticed they completely painted Bernstein in the wrong. I was upset. One of my favorite influencers and someone I loved to support had me rethinking everything and looking more into who I should support and give money.

Bernstein, shortly after, released screenshots of her conversations with the brand Second Wind. They proved she did not steal or solicit designs. Only cropped versions of the conversations were shown, and the story was dramatized to paint Bernstein, once again, in a negative light. Even after sharing the full conversation and receipts, the story was still never updated on the accounts on which it was originally posted.

We're so quick to judge. Humor and stories can spread like wildfire through social media, causing real harm to businesses and people's mental health.

In my life, I've made so many mistakes before, and it's hard for me to think about the pressure of having every move you made watched while starting a business, especially through social media. The more successful you get; the more people want to take you down. When it is too much? Bullying has taken on a whole new level with Instagram, and Bernstein has definitely already experienced it with her body insecurities. Imagine posting a picture of your body in a swimsuit in an attempt to sell that swimsuit line to over two million people? It's scary, and don't think for a second it's not.

We should hold people accountable to being truthful and showing their authentic self without crazy photo editing apps, especially if they're selling a clothing line and people are depending on using you to see how it looks, relying on you to place their order.

If you type into Instagram's search bar "wew..." in searching for Bernstein's main account, you'll see other Instagram accounts pop up—accounts made to bring awareness to Berinstein's photoshopped and edited photos. Some are called "WePhotoShoppedWhat2" and "WeOverWhat." These accounts constantly called out Bernstein for editing her body in photos, comparing photos taken at an event by someone else there to the photos she posted on her feed.

How does anyone have time to put this much energy into bullying any one on social media like this? There are so many bloggers and influencers doing this all the time, and to see it happen on this level is extremely overwhelming. I can't imagine having accounts like this made about myself. I would feel depressed. No one is perfect. We all make mistakes, so should we all be cancelled? Should we rip people to shreds on social media to make a point?

Social media can be a double-edged sword. On one hand, it's great for awareness about your business and as a tool to help your business grow, but on the other hand, you're always going to be watched the more you climb to the top. You have to continue to innovate your brand, but it's important to remember where you came from and never to feel the pressure of being perfect, potentially jeopardizing your brand. Always stay authentic because authenticity equals longevity.

CHAPTER 12

ALMOST (NOT EVEN CLOSE TO) FAMOUS

In 2015, I lived in Washington, D.C., working for a start-up social media agency. At the time, one of my clients was in the travel industry and wanted to explore influencer marketing to promote guests having wonderful experiences at their hotel. The client wanted influencers to show their communities the benefits and perks of my client's hotel versus other competitors' hotels in the area.

As I started researching the best influencers to hire for my client, I became fascinated with how people were starting to create their own personal brand on social media, especially Instagram. Around this time, Instagram had grown to four hundred million monthly active users, so there were a lot of people already on this platform.

As I continued to do research trying to get a price point on how much these influencers would cost for my client, I was shocked to learn after getting in contact with some that rates can range anywhere from five hundred dollars to twenty thousand dollars per post. Influencers charge rates like this depending on a couple different factors, but mainly based on how many followers they have. Back in 2015, a lot of influencer pricing went something like this:[114]

- Facebook's influencer pricing: $25 per one thousand followers
- Instagram's influencer pricing: $10 per one thousand followers
- Snapchat's influencer pricing: $10 per one thousand followers
- YouTube's influencer pricing: $20 per one thousand followers

Most influencers don't share their pricing structures, but this can give you a good baseline for background knowledge. I was thinking to myself: this is crazy. I literally only wanted this person to take a photo outside my client's hotel and post about it with a cheeky caption. That's it, and it didn't seem hard at all. I thought "anyone could do this, right? I could do this and make money from buying clothes I love and sharing them with my friends and followers. Why wasn't I doing this? I mean, taking photos in cute outfits around a city? Sign me up!"

---

114 "Influencer Marketing Pricing: What Does It Cost in 2020?" Webfx.com, accessed August 22, 2020.

SPARK

Later that week, I started figuring out what I could post and what could be a different angle to the brand I wanted to build on social media. I didn't want to put all this time into something someone was already doing. It needed to be different and worth following as a source of content you couldn't get anywhere else. I also had an itch to see what this was all about. Maybe I'll have some fun, get a little "internet famous," and make some extra money on the side.

I started writing down the things I love: bright colors, fashion, clothes, styling, travel, and lots of glitter. I know what you're thinking. Yes, this list is very basic, but if I was going to dedicate extra time to creating a brand, it needed to be a passion of mine. I couldn't stop thinking about the word glitter and how I was already known as the glitter girl in my friend group. A fun fact about me is I used to keep a bag of glitter with me at all times while going out to clubs and bars in D.C. You never know when your night might need a little extra sparkle while out on the town—don't @ me! Glitter was my "extra something"—different from anyone else I knew—and something I needed to convey in my brand.

The more I explored glitter and fashion, I started to see what I wanted to showcase on my account. I wanted to show different designs and outfits inspired by glitter and sequins. My target audience would be someone who enjoys pop culture, daily fashion inspiration, bright colors with a splash of glitz and glamour, and, of course, glitter. I lived in the nation's capital, so there was no better backdrop than my own city for pictures. No one had an account dedicated to this type of fashion, and I was ready to explore it. But there was a big problem. How was I going to support this new passion of mine? I wasn't a trust fund baby with oodles of money to keep buying clothes each week. I needed to get crafty and be strategic with my time since I had a full-time job during the week—that actually paid my bills.

A couple days later, I had a plan in place. I pulled everything out of my closet I could possibly use for photo shoots, created a digital mood board displaying what type of content I would post, and started brainstorming an Instagram username. That afternoon, I got a text from my friend with a picture of us covered in glitter from the night I moved to D.C. We celebrated by pouring glitter on everything and everyone that night, including us. Right after receiving her text, I rushed pulling up Instagram to make sure the name wasn't taken yet, and this was when CoveredNGlitter was born. Unfortunately, CoveredInGlitter was taken, but I made it a little artsy, wouldn't you agree? ;)

SOCIAL MEDIA

There's a demand to keep your audience engaged and entertained on a daily basis. Most influencers on social media post daily, if not multiple times a day. Instagram created Instagram stories, making it easier to create content on the fly and allowing you to create content that isn't so polished at all times. Unfortunately, that tool wasn't available in 2015, leaving me to create editorial content that would live on my front page, so it needed to be perfect. My strategy was to show new, different content as often as possible. I needed to plan out multiple outfit changes because I only had a couple hours to shoot, so I need to make the most of it hoping this content would last for weeks. I decided I would post my original content that I styled one or two times a week while weaving in style inspiration and content from other influencers and celebrities that fit my aesthetic. I also wrote down branded and generic hashtags I could use on my posts to extend the reach of my content. I wanted to showcase lifestyle content that was fun as well as celebratory outfits you could wear no matter the season, all while adding funny memes and relatable content into the mix.

As I was looking at the items pulled out of my closet, I started to group them (clothes, shoes, accessories, jewelry) into different categories, creating a content theme for my first couple of posts. This also helped me with my editorial plan and in figuring out a posting cadence I could visualize. It helped me stay organized when managing my channel to easily see what and when I needed to post. I knew I needed to be "on trend" with buying new pieces to display on my profile, so I listed out a couple different stores I knew had a great return policy. I couldn't afford to keep all of the clothes, so I would pick out pieces, keep the tags on them while shooting in the clothes, and after, collecting this content, return the clothes.

Technically I wasn't "wearing" it out, just taking a photo in the outfit. Was this wrong? Right or wrong, it's the truth of what I did. Most influencers starting in a similar space probably wouldn't admit this, but most who didn't come from money used the same, if not similar, methods in the beginning. Once I picked out my favorite glittery pieces from the store, I returned home and styled the clothes with my own accessories. From there, I would line up all the outfits I planned to shoot in, organizing and grouping each look from head to toe, and load everything into the car.

Once I had everything ready to go, I needed someone to help me shoot content. I didn't have enough money for a model, so I became the model. My boyfriend at the time, and now husband, had just purchased a beautiful camera he was stoked to try out. I asked, begged, if he'd help me out for a couple of shoots until I figured out something more permanent. Being the good human he is, he agreed to help.

The night before we planned to go out on our first adventure, I made a list of DC's iconic places I wanted to use as my backdrop for the content I was creating. I also needed to pack every single outfit into the car because most of the places we were going to didn't have bathrooms close by. If you saw someone on the mall in a 2007 white Honda CR-V in DC back in 2015 changing into the brightest, most sparkly outfits ever, that was me!

The morning came, so we packed up and headed straight to the Washington Monument for our first shoot. We had less than ten minutes to capture what we needed because we didn't want to pay for parking since we intended to not be there for long. However, the process took so much longer than I anticipated. Not only does it take time to capture great content, but you have to adjust the camera settings, make sure people aren't walking by and/or ruining your shot, and deal with unexpected traffic and tourists in the city. Five location shoots and six hours later, we returned home, exhausted and tired, but I was just getting started.

Once we uploaded all the photos, we realized there were over four thousand images to pick from. It took me hours to sort through the photos, condensing down to the ones I'd use on my channel. After that, I needed to edit them and start thinking of copy ideas to go along with my photos. Have you ever taken a stellar photo for social media and wanted the perfect copy to go along with it? Well, if you have, then you know it takes FOREVER (or at least for me). Now, I had to come up with captions for over one hundred photos. I already poured in hours of blood, sweat, and tears into this, and I still had not posted a single photo yet. I couldn't believe the amount of planning, time, and energy that already went into this, but I had my mind set to at least give this a couple of months to see where it could go.

Once I had all my assets together (including the first image I wanted to post), my Instagram handle secured, and a really cool caption to kick off my new brand, (we were live), I was that much closer to "influencer" famous... a girl can dream, right?

SECRET SAUCE

After weeks of trying to keep this account together, I realized how hard becoming an influencer actually was. I spent countless hours creating content, shooting, editing, copywriting, branding, etc.— things I thought would take a couple hours maximum each week. My so-called "hobby," supposedly a fun journey of exploring the influencer marketing world, turned to be nothing as I expected. I wasn't seeing any growth on my channel. The obvious fans, like sweet family and friends giving me a courtesy follow, were nice, but I didn't experience the growth I expected considering the incredibly thought-provoking content I was putting out into the world. It was depressing to see the insight results on each post, knowing how much time and dedication went into each piece of content. What was I doing wrong? I spent HOURS, and I mean HOURS, running around perfecting this content. I thought I'd had this in the bag? After all, I was doing all the right things each week:

- Constantly creating new content weekly, if not daily
- Running to stores to shop and pick out looks to style
- Styling multiple outfits at a time
- Spending hours shooting and editing the content I captured
- Researching potential brand partnerships for future collaborations
- Staying up-to-date on the latest fashion trends to post relevant content
- Researching hashtags and which ones I should use
- Posting daily and coming up with creative captions
- Creating social media campaigns, like giveaways, to feature

And those are just some of the things I did. I quickly realized why influencers charge the rate they do. Growing a brand takes time as well as consistency. Not only does it involve a lot of time, but money, skills, resourcefulness, creativity, and quick problem solving are also required to find ways around difficult challenges. I also found I might not be a good influencer in persuading people's purchasing decisions. People might not gravitate to the content I put out.

36
Posts

72
Followers

262
Following

Digital Creator
 Not your average hype women
Daily motivation from one girl boss to the next.
Don't let anyone ever dull your sparkle.

Edit Profile   **Promotions**   **Insights**

After posting for a while, I noticed my account became more of a personal inspiration mood board for me. I wasn't thinking about what content people would like; instead, I was thinking about the content I liked, hoping other people would like it too. People don't understand that when you're creating a brand, or even a personal brand, the secret sauce to the formula is figuring out a niche in the market consumers want that doesn't exist yet. Sure, I looked at similar profiles on Instagram to make sure mine stood out and was different, but I realized I never looked to see if there was a community that was craving this type of content. You could argue people don't know what they want until you show them, but if that's the case, then whatever you're showing a consumer needs to fix a current problem they're facing, a problem they never knew about until discovering you.

SUCCESS?

Through my own personal journey becoming an influencer, my whole perception changed about influencer culture. I learned how much is involved in the process and how everyone isn't meant to be an influencer. There's a certain list of requirements and skills you need in order to achieve the same level of success as some of the women we talked about in this book, and I realized I wasn't dedicated to the practice enough. Even though I wasn't successful at becoming an influencer, I realized my unique ability is to help other brands build their communities. After all, you must build credibility in order to achieve the next step up.

CONCLUSION

Self-development is a continuous journey of trial and error. The process will test your strengths, reveal your weaknesses, and empower you to put yourself (finally) first. Keep going, no matter what. Dive deep into answering the questions that you currently refuse to discover, no matter how much the answer hurts. Be honest, be open, and be less critical of yourself. You deserve respect and understanding in the process of self-discovery. Today, I hope this reminder serves you well—to help you know that we are all in this together, on a journey of self-discovery and growth.

BY TIFFANY MOULE

Originally, I wrote this book for me, but I've already gotten benefit out of it in learning from these "Voguepreneurs." So now, I hope you have benefitted from this book, too. I hope these stories of taking chances, putting in hard work, and going after your dreams motivate you to take the next step in your own life.

Hopefully, throughout this book, you've learned something you didn't already know, laughed, or felt motivated to start your own digital brand, whether becoming an influencer or creating a company through your own digital efforts.

In almost every job I've had, I've felt like I've hit the glass ceiling, and I wasn't sure what to do nor where to turn. I switched career paths in my mid-twenties from event planning to focusing my time and energy in social media advertising. After being at one of the top social media agencies for almost three years, I felt like more needed to be said about how women were using social media to break glass ceilings and create their own futures.

At the end of 2019, I applied for a job I really wanted.

The position was in the tech industry, a totally new category in which I didn't have a ton of experience, but knew I could learn about fast. With Raleigh rapidly growing in this field with more tech companies coming to the area, I knew I wanted to be a part of it and make my mark in a new category—something I was totally ready for. After the final interview, I was so confident I landed the job. I was even starting to make plans on my new commute and what I was planning to tell my current co-workers; it was all mapped out.

After patiently waiting a week, I received a voicemail on my phone after a sync with my manager where I currently worked at the time. I couldn't get out of the door fast enough to hear what the voicemail said. The voice in my head was saying, "there's no way they'd leave a rejection voicemail on my phone, right?" As soon as I started playing the voicemail and heard the words "Everyone had positive feedback but …" I felt my heart beating out of my chest. The recruiter told me they ultimately chose to go with another candidate. My heart broke into a million pieces, and from that point on, I told myself that I was going to take my career to the next level, proving to myself I can do anything I set my mind to. I started thinking: what could I possibly do without completely starting over? I knew I wanted to keep my focus in digital marketing, but how could I show my thought leadership in this growing industry?

Rewind another year, back to 2018. I was sitting in bed trying to wake up from a nap when my husband, Stu, dropped a huge bomb on me. "Honey, I'm going to write a book." My initial response was "Uh, yeah … okay," but he replied "No, seriously … this is how I'm going to take my passion and career to the next level." He pulled up a video of Professor Koester, a professor who turned his Entrepreneur 101 class at Georgetown University into a class ending with each student publishing a written book. Based on Professor Koester's innovative research, he found success doesn't automatically come from prestigious degrees or high-profile jobs. Success comes from what we create and how we credibly demonstrate our expertise.[115] Today's most successful young people build their own credibility through books, podcasts, event series,

---

115 "Creator Institute | Learn Through Creating Your Book | Why." Creator-Institute, accessed August 22, 2020.

research, and more. The class is designed to enable each person to do the same to achieve their goals.

When my husband told me all of this, I was skeptical of the process, thinking this was just something he could put on his resume. Well, I was partially right, as he could add this to his LinkedIn profile and resume, but the surprising parts were the quality of people he spoke with, the doors opened for him, and the fact that he could brag about writing a freaking BOOK. I had no idea how hard it would actually be, but he showed me he could do it, giving me the inspiration and push I needed.

After the negative voicemail for what I thought would be my next dream job, I took a day to cry it out and push my frustrations aside, and then got to work. One week later, Stu sent an introduction email to Professor Koester, and the rest is history. While I'm scared that no one will read this book or people will judge me for putting my thoughts and ideas out there, writing this book showed me if you set your mind to believing you can achieve success, then you can. If you believe something is too out of reach, it's not, because you're just telling yourself that lie. Because of these self-doubting thoughts, we feel behind in life—either personally or professionally. For a while, I've felt behind in life professionally. That feeling is a huge reason why I started writing this book— to challenge myself to achieve something I never thought would be possible.

In envisioning my life by the time I turned thirty, I'd thought there would always be someone—a leader or a mentor—to show me the ropes and guide me through the hurdles of "corporate America." The truth is, we're not behind in life. There is no timetable we all must follow. Everyone grows at a difference pace. Sometimes when we get to a door, it's locked for a reason. You'll eventually find an unlocked door meant for you to open, walk through, and follow its path to see where it leads you—just like all these women who have broken boundaries and reshaped billion-dollar industries. These are my "digital" mentors, my leaders, and the women I look up to. Which "bosses" do you really connect with online, and what lessons can you learn from them, even if you've never met them in person?

I guess in a way, I needed to write this book for it to be my own guide to success. How all of these women have paved their own path is inspiring, and we can all take a page out of their book and learn something to apply to our own lives.

We all have our own stories, and this is mine. How will you write yours?

ACKNOWLEDGEMENT

———

Stu, my schnug, thank you for pushing me to write on weekends when all I wanted to do was go to brunch. Even on my hardest days, you always encouraged me to write and finish this book when I would try and find every excuse not to. Thank you for being my biggest fan, my rock, and my support system through completing one of the biggest accomplishments in my life.

Mom and Dad, thank you for always loving and supporting me. There wasn't a parenting book in the world that would have prepared you for me, but I feel like I turned out alright.

And to all the strong women in my life who don't give up on their dreams, don't take anything personally, and don't take no for an answer, this book is for you.

INDIEGOGO ACKNOWLEDGEMENTS:

A special thank you to my biggest IndieGoGo campaign supports who helped make this book possible:

The Arkys, The Crudups, Christine Wilson, Natalie Viniotis, The Strauchs, The Costins, Kraig and Cece Siracuse

APPENDIX

———

INTRODUCTION

Business Insider. "The Influencer Marketing Report." *Business Insider Intelligence Research Store*. 2019. (accessed March 28, 2020). https://store.businessinsider.com/products/the-influencer-marketing-report.

"Influencer Marketing Stats | 80 Influencer Marketing Statistics For 2020." *Influencer Marketing Hub*. 2020. (accessed March 28, 2020). https://influencermarketinghub.com/influencer-marketing-statistics/.

HISTORY OF DIGITAL

"16 LinkedIn Statistics That Matter to Marketers in 2019." Social Media Marketing & Management Dashboard. March 9, 2020. (accessed March 28, 2020). https://blog.hootsuite.com/linkedin-statistics-business/.

Abbruzzese, Jason. "The Rise And Fall Of AIM, The Breakthrough AOL Never Wanted." *Mashable*. 2014. (accessed March 28, 2020). https://mashable.com/2014/04/15/aim-history/.

"About LinkedIn." Linkedin.Com. About LinkedIn. 2016. (accessed March 28, 2020). https://about.linkedin.com/.

Andrews, Travis. "Charli D'Amelio Is TikTok's Biggest Star. She Has No Idea Why." *The Washington Post*. May 26, 2020. (accessed March 28, 2020). https://www.washingtonpost.com/technology/2020/05/26/charli-damelio-tiktok-star/?arc404=true.

Bernazzani, Sophia. "A Brief History of Snapchat." Hubspot.Com. 2012. (accessed March 28, 2020). https://blog.hubspot.com/marketing/history-of-snapchat.

"ByteDance." Bytedance.Com. 2012. (accessed March 28, 2020). https://www.bytedance.com/en/products.

Carlson, Nicholas. "The Real History Of Twitter - Business Insider." Business Insider. Business Insider. April 13, 2011. 2011. (accessed March 28, 2020). https://www.businessinsider.com/how-twitter-was-founded-2011-4.

Clement, J. "Digital Users Worldwide 2020 | Statista." *Statista*. 2020 (accessed March 28, 2020). https://www.statista.com/statistics/617136/digital-population-worldwide/.

"Facebook Overtakes MySpace in U.S." PCWorld. June 16, 2009. (accessed March 28, 2020). https://www.pcworld.com/article/166794/Facebook_Overtakes_MySpace_in_US.html#:~:-

text=Facebook%20has%20officially%20taken%20the,by%20
Web%20metrics%20firm%20ComScore.

"Fisher, Adam.""Google Was Not A Normal Place": Brin, Page, And Mayer On The Accidental Birth Of The Company That Changed Everything." *Vanity Fair.* 2018. (accessed March 28, 2020). https://www.vanityfair.com/news/2018/07/valley-of-genius-excerpt-google.

Fox, Chris. "Twitter Axes Vine Video Service." BBC News. BBC News. October 27, 2016. (accessed March 28, 2020). https://www.bbc.com/news/technology-37788052.

Jones, Dow. "COMPANY NEWS; YOUTHSTREAM TO ACQUIRE SIXDEGREES FOR $125 MILLION." *Nytimes. Com.* December 16, 1999. (accessed March 28, 2020). https://www.nytimes.com/1999/12/16/business/company-news-youth-stream-to-acquire-sixdegrees-for-125-million.html.

Matsakis, Louise. "How to Use TikTok: Tips for New Users." Wired. WIRED. March 6, 2019. (accessed March 28, 2020). https://www.wired.com/story/how-to-use-tik-tok/.

Newton, Casey. "Facebook Announces Video for Instagram." The Verge. The Verge. June 20, 2013. (accessed March 28, 2020). https://www.theverge.com/2013/6/20/4448182/facebook.

Newton, Casey. "Why Vine Died." The Verge. The Verge. October 28, 2016. (accessed March 28, 2020). https://www.theverge.com/2016/10/28/13456208/why-vine-died-twitter-shutdown.

Perlberg, Steven, and Shields, Mike. "Vine Stars Are Leaving for Facebook and Other Platforms." WSJ. The Wall Street Journal. May 13, 2016. (accessed March 28, 2020). https://www.wsj.com/articles/video-stars-are-withering-on-the-vine-1463152655.

Peters, Meghan. "internet Surpasses Television as Main News Source for Young Adults [STUDY]." Mashable. January 4, 2011. (accessed March 28, 2020). https://mashable.com/2011/01/04/internet-surpasses-television-as-main-news-source-for-young-adults-study/.

Rusli, Evelyn M. "Facebook Buys Instagram for $1 Billion." DealBook. May 16, 2012. (accessed March 28, 2020). https://dealbook.nytimes.com/2012/04/09/facebook-buys-instagram-for-1-billion/.

"Sponsored InMail Best Practices & Gallery of Examples." n.d. (Accessed August 30, 2020). https://business.linkedin.com/content/dam/me/business/en-us/marketing-solutions/cx/2016/pdfs/Sponsored-InMail-Best-Practices-pilot.pdf.

"The Associated Press. "Timeline: Key Dates in Facebook's 10-Year History." Phys.Org. Phys.org. February 4, 2014. (accessed March 28, 2020). https://phys.org/news/2014-02-timeline-key-dates-facebook-year.html.

"Then And Now: A History Of Social Networking Sites." Cbsnews. Com. 2020. (accessed March 28, 2020). https://www.cbsnews.com/pictures/then-and-now-a-history-of-social-networking-sites/2/.

FROM HOLLYWOOD SOCIALITIES TO DIGITAL INFLUENCERS

By Dailymail.com Reporter. 2019. "Kim Kardashian Says Paris Hilton 'gave Me a Career' as She Reunites with Old Friend." Mail Online. Daily Mail. October 14, 2019. (accessed March 28, 2020).https://www.dailymail.co.uk/tvshowbiz/article-7572179/Kim-Kardashian-says-Paris-Hilton-gave-career-reunites-old-friend.html.

Duboff, Josh. 2015. "Blake Lively's Preserve: An Obituary." Vanity Fair. Vanity Fair. September 30, 2015. (accessed March 28, 2020). https://www.vanityfair.com/style/2015/09/blake-lively-preserve-shutting-down.

Foley, Rachel. 2019. "Kylie Jenner: Is She Really a 'self-Made' Billionaire?" *BBC News*, March 6, 2019. (accessed March 28, 2020). https://www.bbc.com/news/entertainment-arts-47468641.

Michael, Alex. 2017. "Inside Paris Hilton's Multi-Billion Dollar Retail Empire." Mail Online. Daily Mail. November 29, 2017. (accessed March 28, 2020). https://www.dailymail.co.uk/tvshowbiz/article-5127225/Inside-Paris-Hiltons-multi-billion-dollar-retail-empire.html.

Moran, Justin. 2018. "How Paris Hilton Invented the Social Media Star." PAPER. PAPER. April 27, 2018. (accessed March 28, 2020). https://www.papermag.com/paris-hilton-american-meme-2563903322.html.

Peterson-Withorn, Chase. 2020. "Kylie Jenner Is Still The Youngest Self-Made Billionaire In The World." *Forbes*, April 7, 2020. (accessed March 28, 2020). https://www.forbes.com/sites/

chasewithorn/2020/04/07/kylie-jenner-is-still-the-youngest-self-made-billionaire-in-the-world/#d1d1f02198bc.

Russo, Maria. 2008. "Just a Bunch of Goop." Baltimoresun.Com. September 30, 2008. (accessed March 28, 2020). https://www.baltimoresun.com/news/bs-xpm-2008-09-30-0809290094-story.html.

Sharkey, Alix. 2006. "David LaChapelle: Maximum Exposure." The Guardian. The Guardian. February 5, 2006. (accessed March 28, 2020). https://www.theguardian.com/film/2006/feb/05/features.magazine.

Shaw, Gabbi. 2019. "31 Celebrities Who Tried — and Failed — to Start Their Own Businesses - Insider." Insider. Insider. June 20, 2019. (accessed March 28, 2020). https://www.insider.com/celebrity-business-fails-2018-6.

Simon, Dan. 2014. "'Ditzy Blonde' No More: Paris Hilton Reinvents Herself As A Serious Entrepreneur -- And Crushes It." *Forbes*, June 5, 2014. (accessed March 28, 2020). https://www.forbes.com/sites/dansimon/2014/06/04/paris-in-the-springtime-the-caricatured-ditzy-blonde-reinvents-herself-as-serious-entrepreneur-and-crushes-it/#70b104de133f.

THE RISE OF INFLUENCER MARKETING

"Influencer Marketing Predictions for 2020 - Top Industry Experts Weigh In." Influencer Marketing Hub. January 3, 2020. (accessed March 28, 2020). https://influencermarketinghub.com/influencer-marketing-predictions-2020/.

"Lord & Taylor Settles FTC Charges It Deceived Consumers Through Paid Article in an Online Fashion Magazine and Paid Instagram Posts by 50 'Fashion Influencers.'" Federal Trade Commission. March 15, 2016. (accessed March 28, 2020). https://www.ftc.gov/news-events/press-releases/2016/03/lord-taylor-settles-ftc-charges-it-deceived-consumers-through.

"37 Instagram Statistics That Matter to Marketers in 2020." Social Media Marketing & Management Dashboard. October 22, 2019. (accessed March 28, 2020). https://blog.hootsuite.com/instagram-statistics/.

Brooks, Aaron. "[Timeline] A Brief History of Influencers." Social Media Today. May 9, 2019. (accessed March 28, 2020). https://www.socialmediatoday.com/news/timeline-a-brief-history-of-influencers/554377/.

Hausman, Angela. "The Rise and Fall of the Social Media Influencer." Marketing Insider Group. January 17, 2019. (accessed March 28, 2020). https://marketinginsidergroup.com/influencer-marketing/the-rise-and-fall-of-the-social-media-influencer/.

"Kerrigan, Serena" Serena Kerrigan, Accessed August 22, 2020. https://www.serenakerrigan.com/about.

BRICK-AND-MORTAR TO DIGITAL STOREFRONTS

"Average Time Spent Daily on Social Media (Latest 2020 Data)." 2020. BroadbandSearch.Net. 2020. (accessed March 28, 2020). https://www.broadbandsearch.net/blog/average-daily-time-on-social-media.

Belluz, Julia. 2018. "Gwyneth Paltrow Split with Condé Nast over Fact-Checking." Vox. Vox. July 26, 2018. (accessed March 28, 2020). https://www.vox.com/science-and-health/2018/7/26/17616792/gwyneth-paltrow-goop-fact-checker.

Clevver News. 2016. "Kylie Jenner Builds A Crazy Wall of Lip Kits for Pop-Up Shop." YouTube Video. *YouTube.* https://www.youtube.com/watch?v=FOjebRtP4xc.

Creeden, Molly. 2016. "Gwyneth Paltrow Introduces Goop by Juice Beauty Skin Care." Vogue. Vogue. January 20, 2016. (accessed March 28, 2020). https://www.vogue.com/article/gwyneth-paltrow-goop-by-juice-beauty-skin-care-announcement.

"Digital 2020: 3.8 Billion People Use Social Media - We Are Social." 2020. We Are Social. January 30, 2020. (accessed March 28, 2020). https://wearesocial.com/blog/2020/01/digital-2020-3-8-billion-people-use-social-media#:~:text=Nearly%2060%20percent%20of%20the,the%20middle%20of%20this%20year.

DMI, Simon. 2017. "9 Ways Digital Has Changed Business Forever." Digital Marketing Institute. Digital Marketing Institute. April 14, 2017. (accessed March 28, 2020). https://digitalmarketinginstitute.com/blog/9-ways-digital-has-changed-business-forever.

Fallon, Jimmy. 2016. "Gwyneth Paltrow and Jimmy Eat Her Goop Skincare Line." YouTube Video. YouTube. (accessed March 28, 2020). https://www.youtube.com/watch?v=IVD_OLALP18.

"Instagram Shopping: Does It Work? (It Does For These Brands)." The BigCommerce Blog. March 20, 2018. (accessed March 28,

2020). https://www.bigcommerce.com/blog/instagram-shopping/.

Matney, Lucas. 2020. "Snapchat Boosts Its AR Platform with Voice Search, Local Lenses and SnapML." TechCrunch. TechCrunch. June 11, 2020. (accessed March 28, 2020). https://techcrunch.com/2020/06/11/snapchat-boosts-its-ar-platform-with-voice-search-local-lenses-and-snapml/.

Sanderson, Rachel. 2019. "Chiara Ferragni — the Italian Influencer Who Built a Global Brand." @FinancialTimes. Financial Times. February 8, 2019. (accessed March 28, 2020). https://www.ft.com/content/9adce87c-2879-11e9-a5ab-ff8ef2b976c7.

"Spectacles by Snap Inc. Capture Your World in 3D." 2020. Spectacles.Com. 2020. https://www.spectacles.com/.

"Why Is Chiara Ferragni Famous?" 2020. A Day in the Life. A Day in the Life. March 2, 2020. (accessed March 28, 2020). https://mdmartina.art.blog/2020/03/02/why-is-chiara-ferragni-famous/.

4S PROCESS

Carbone, Lexie. "Ultimate Guide to Instagram For Fashion: Content, Analytics, Influencers, & More!" Later Blog. May 9, 2019. (accessed March 28, 2020). https://later.com/blog/instagram-for-fashion/#success.

Eldor, Karin. "How 'Sincerely Jules' Parlayed Her 5.5M Instagram Followers Into Billabong's Most Successful Collab." *Forbes*, March 13, 2020. (accessed March 28, 2020). https://www.forbes.

com/sites/karineldor/2020/03/13/how-julie-sarinana-of-sincerely-jules-parlayed-her-55m-instagram-followers-into-billabongs-most-successful-collab/#64a001ce61bd.

"Fenty Beauty by Rihanna | About | Fenty Beauty." Fenty Beauty. 2020. (accessed March 28, 2020). https://www.fentybeauty.com/about-fenty#:~:text=Rihanna%20was%20inspired%20to%20create,all%20skin%20types%20and%20tones.

Fowler, Brandi. "Style Influencer Sincerely Jules on the Biggest Splurge Item in Her Closet." InStyle.Com. InStyle. March 21, 2019. (accessed March 28, 2020). https://www.instyle.com/reviews-coverage/social-media/money-talks-julie-sarinana.

Hutcheson, Susannah. "How I Became a Makeup Mogul: Beauty Influencer Huda Kattan Talks about Business, Life." USA TODAY. USA TODAY. August 21, 2018. (accessed March 28, 2020). https://www.usatoday.com/story/money/careers/getting-started/2018/08/21/beauty-influencer-huda-kattan-how-became-makeup-mogul/1040304002/.

Ifeanyi, K.C. "How Huda Kattan Built a Multi-Million-Dollar Beauty Brand from a Blog." Fast Company. Fast Company. July 9, 2018. (accessed March 28, 2020). https://www.fastcompany.com/90180015/how-huda-kattan-built-a-multi-million-dollar-beauty-brand-from-a-blog.

Null. "Why It's Rihanna's World." Grazia. Grazia. November 28, 2017. (accessed March 28, 2020). https://graziadaily.co.uk/beauty-hair/makeup/rihanna-world/.

Schomer, Audrey. "Influencer Marketing: State of the Social Media Influencer Market in 2020 - Business Insider." Business Insider. Business Insider. December 17, 2019. (accessed March 28, 2020). https://www.businessinsider.com/influencer-marketing-report.

THE SPARK – HOW TO FIND YOUR UNIQUE VOICE

Guardian staff reporter. "Pat McGrath Labs Becomes Selfridges Biggest-Selling Beauty Line." The Guardian. The Guardian. June 2019. (accessed August 1, 2020). https://www.theguardian.com/fashion/2019/jun/01/pat-mcgrath-labs-becomes-selfridges-biggest-selling-beauty-line.

Lang, Cady. "How Renowned Makeup Artist Pat McGrath Is Changing the Face of Beauty On Her Terms." Time.Com. Time. September 18, 2017. (accessed August 1, 2020). https://time.com/4945033/pat-mcgrath-unlimited-interview/.

McGrath, Pat. "Pat McGrath Is Part of the BoF 500." The Business of Fashion. April 27, 2019. (accessed August 1, 2020). https://www.businessoffashion.com/community/people/pat-mcgrath#:~:text=British%20makeup%20artist%20Pat%20McGrath,world's%20most%20important%20makeup%20artist.&text=Born%20and%20raised%20in%20Northampton,-shows%2C%20right%20there.

Redazione. "How Pat McGrath Built a Sell-out Beauty Brand for the Instagram Age." Vogue.It. Vogue. July 28, 2017. (accessed August 1, 2020). https://www.vogue.it/en/beauty-look/news/2017/07/28/pat-mcgrath-labs-secrets-successful-beauty-brand-instagram-age/?refresh_ce=.

Saltzman, Stephanie. "Pat McGrath on Why Diversity and Inclusivity Have Been Crucial to Her Brand From Its Launch." Fashionista. August 16, 2018. (accessed August 1, 2020). https://fashionista.com/2018/08/pat-mcgrath-labs-makeup-diversity-inclusivity.

HOW SOCIAL MEDIA PRESENCE IS EVERYTHING

McCall, Tyler. 2019. "How Katie Sturino Went from Working in PR to Becoming an Influencer-Entrepreneur." Fashionista. September 17, 2019. (accessed August 22, 2020). https://fashionista.com/2019/09/katie-sturino-stitch-fix-megababe.

Rodulfo, Kristina. 2019. "Megababe Has Solutions for Beauty Problems We Don't Talk About. They Sell Out Immediately." ELLE. ELLE. January 28, 2019. (accessed August 22, 2020). https://www.elle.com/beauty/makeup-skin-care/a26009547/megababe-katie-sturino/.

SECRET SAUCE – THE POWER OF INFLUENCE

Bernstein, Danielle, and Sigel, This Is Not a Fashion Story: Taking Chances, Breaking Rules, and Being a Boss in the Big City (North Charleston, Vertel Publishing, 2020).

Coghlan, Claire. 2017. "How 'We Wore What' Blogger Danielle Bernstein Went From Sophomore To Seven Figures In Under 6 Years." Forbes, August 23, 2017. (accessed August 22, 2020). https://www.forbes.com/sites/clairecoghlan/2017/08/23/how-we-wore-what-blogger-danielle-bernstein-went-from-sophomore-to-seven-figures-in-under-6-years/#5de5160d5843.

Roche, Eddie. 2019. "Danielle Bernstein Gets Real About Money And The Power of Influence." Daily Front Row. Daily Front Row. February 11, 2019. (accessed August 22, 2020). https://fashionweekdaily.com/danielle-bernstein-fashion-influencer/.

SUCCESS — GROW YOUR BRAND AND START WINNING

"#glossierpink Hashtag on Instagram" Instagram.Com. 2018. (accessed March 28, 2020). https://www.instagram.com/explore/tags/glossierpink/?hl=en.

"#ITGTopShelfie Archives - Into The Gloss." Into The Gloss. 2020. (accessed March 28, 2020). https://intothegloss.com/categories/itgtopshelfie-2/.

Fior Market Research LLP. "Global Beauty and Personal Care Product Market Is Expected to Reach USD 756.63 Billion by 2026 : Fior Markets." GlobeNewswire News Room. January 24, 2020. (accessed March 28, 2020). https://www.globenewswire.com/news-release/2020/01/24/1974743/0/en/Global-Beauty-and-Personal-Care-Product-Market-is-Expected-to-Reach-USD-756-63-Billion-by-2026-Fior-Markets.html.

Forrester, Joele. "60% of Marketers Say Influencer Budgets Will Stay the Same or Increase Post-COVID-19 - [Talking Influence]." May 28, 2020. (accessed March 28, 2020). https://talkinginfluence.com/2020/05/28/covid-19-impacted-98-influencer-strategies/.

Hart, Kaley. "The Glossier Marketing Machine: How Emily Weiss Hacked Culture to Build a $100 Million Business That's Disrupting Beauty." Jumper Media. Jumper Media. February 22,

2019. (accessed March 28, 2020). https://jumpermedia.co/gloss-ier-marketing-machine/.

"How Glossier Turned Into a $400 Million Business in Four Years." Product Habits. May 28, 2018. (accessed March 28, 2020). https://producthabits.com/how-glossier-turned-into-a-400-million-business-in-four-years/.

McCall, Tyler. "A Decade in Digital: Emily Weiss Wants Into the Gloss and Glossier to Be About More than Product." Fashionista. September 18, 2017. (accessed March 28, 2020). https://fashionista.com/2017/09/emily-weiss-glossier-interview.

Murray, Becki. "Glossier Is Launching a New Brow Product to Accompany Boy Brow." Harper's BAZAAR. Harper's BAZAAR. June 12, 2019. (accessed March 28, 2020). https://www.harpersbazaar.com/uk/beauty/make-up-nails/a27583020/glossiers-new-brow.

Schawbel, Dan. "10 New Findings About The Millennial Consumer." *Forbes*, January 20, 2015. (accessed March 28, 2020). https://www.forbes.com/sites/danschawbel/2015/01/20/10-new-findings-about-the-millennial-consumer/#71b694586c8f.

FUTURE OF DIGITAL

Barker, Shane. 2020. "The Future of Social Media Marketing – 11 Trends That Will Impact Your Business (Updated May 2020)." Shane Barker. Shane Barker. (Updated May 2020). May 18, 2020. (accessed August 22, 2020). https://shanebarker.com/blog/future-of-social-media-marketing/.

"The Most Important Social Media Trends to Know for 2020."
Sprout Social. August 4, 2020. (accessed August 22, 2020).
https://sproutsocial.com/insights/social-media-trends/.

"US Time Spent with Media 2020." 2020. EMarketer. (accessed
August 22, 2020). https://www.emarketer.com/content/
us-time-spent-with-media-2020.

"Why Brands Need to Have an Augmented Reality Plan to Reach
Young Consumers – YPulse." 2020. Ypulse.Com. 2020.
(accessed August 22, 2020). https://www.ypulse.com/arti-
cle/2020/05/14/why-brands-need-to-have-an-augmented-re-
ality-plan-to-reach-young-consumers/.

CANCELLING "CANCEL CULTURE"

Beswick, Sedge. "How Can Brands Working with Influencers
Safeguard against 'Cancel Culture.'" The Drum. The Drum.
March 16, 2020. (accessed August 22, 2020). https://www.the-
drum.com/opinion/2020/03/16/how-can-brands-working-
with-influencers-safeguard-against-cancel-culture.

Dictionary.com. "Cancel Culture." Dictionary.Com. Dictionary.
com. July 31, 2020. (accessed August 22, 2020). https://www.
dictionary.com/e/pop-culture/cancel-culture/.

"What Indie Beauty Brand Founders Make Of Cancel Culture -
Beauty Independent." 2020. Beauty Independent. July 29, 2020.
(accessed August 22, 2020). https://www.beautyindependent.
com/what-indie-beauty-brand-founders-make-of-cancel-cul-
ture/.

The New York Times. "We're All Drinking Diet Prada Now,"
March 14, 2019. (accessed August 22, 2020). https://www.
nytimes.com/2019/03/14/fashion/diet-prada.html.

ALMOST (NOT EVEN CLOSE) FAMOUS

"Influencer Marketing Pricing: What Does It Cost in 2020?" 2020.
Webfx.Com. 2020. (accessed August 22, 2020). https://www.
webfx.com/influencer-marketing-pricing.html.

CONCLUSION

"Creator Institute | Learn Through Creating Your Book | Why."
Creator-Institute. 2016. (accessed August 22, 2020). https://
www.creator.institute/about-class.

CPSIA information can be obtained
at www.ICGtesting.com
Printed in the USA
BVHW041811201220
596043BV00008B/20

9 781636 765051